Allie' s

Amish Family Miracle

THE AMISH WOMEN OF
LAWRENCE COUNTY SERIES - BOOK 5

Tracy Fredrychowski

ISBN: 979-8-9879040-2-2 (paperback)

ISBN: 979-8-9879040-1-5 (digital)

Published in South Carolina by The Tracer Group, LLC

https://tracyfredrychowski.com

I dedicate this book to my dear friends Mel and Barb Beechy whom I very loosely modeled this story after. May their love and determination continue to be a source of inspiration for their family for generations to come.

By Tracy Fredrychowski

AMISH OF LAWRENCE COUNTY SERIES

Secrets of Willow Springs – Book 1

Secrets of Willow Springs – Book 2

Secrets of Willow Springs – Book 3

APPLE BLOSSOM INN SERIES

Love Blooms at the Apple Blossom Inn

An Amish Christmas at the Apple Blossom Inn

NOVELLA'S

The Amish Women of Lawrence County

An Amish Gift Worth Waiting For

The Orphans' Amish Christmas

THE AMISH WOMEN OF LAWRENCE COUNTY

Emma's Amish Faith Tested – Book 1

Rebecca's Amish Heart Restored – Book 2

Anna's Amish Fears Revealed – Book 3

Barbara's Amish Truth Exposed – Book 4

Allie's Amish Family Miracle – Book 5

www.tracyfredrychowski.com

Contents

A NOTE ABOUT AMISH VOCABULARY

The Amish language is called Pennsylvania Dutch and is usually spoken rather than written. The spelling of commonly used words varies from community to community throughout the United States and Canada. Even as I researched this book, some words' spelling changed within the same Amish community that inspired this story. In one case, spellings were debated between family members. Some of the terms may have slightly different spellings. Still, all came from my interactions with the Amish settlement near where I was raised in northwestern Pennsylvania.

While this book was modeled upon a small community in Lawrence County, this is a work of fiction. The names and characters are products of my imagination. They do not resemble any person, living or dead, or actual events in that community.

LIST OF CHARACTERS

Allie Mast. Young Mennonite woman from Sugarcreek who moves to Willow Springs to help in her aunts' dry goods store.

Reuben Raber. Youngest male in the Raber family who goes against tradition by falling in love with someone outside his church district.

Saloma Raber. Domineering mother who does all she can to keep her youngest from leaving his Amish roots.

Daniel Raber. Quiet and reserved head of the Raber family.

Elwin Raber. Reuben's wild Amish cousin.

Lydia Kurtz. Allie's wise and encouraging older neighbor.

Virginia Yoder. Saloma's choice for Reuben's *fraa*.

Mose & Catherine Weaver. District bishop and longtime friends of Saloma and Daniel Raber.

MAP OF WILLOW SPRINGS

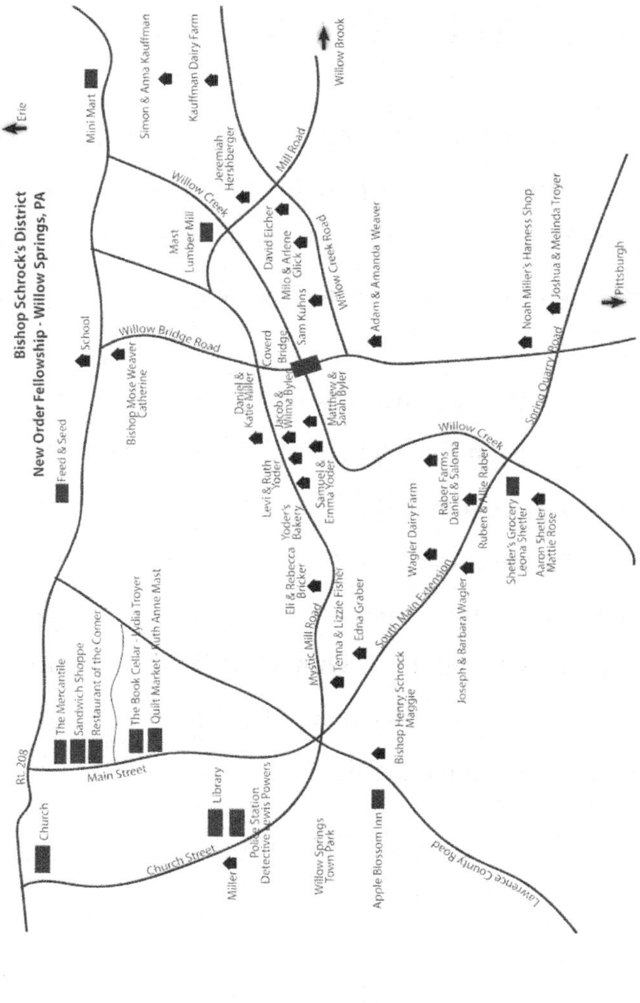

PROLOGUE

Willow Springs, Pennsylvania

Allie Raber

Every family is different, and I realize that, but I never dreamed I'd find myself at odds with my husband's mother like I am. The woman just infuriates me. Her overbearing claim to control every aspect of our life pushes me to my limit.

The good Lord knows I've spent many days begging Him to give me the power of wisdom and understanding to deal with her. Still, Saloma Raber is like no other woman I've ever met.

The mere thought of her bossy disposition and her unnerving habit of having to have the last word drives a wedge between

Reuben and I. We've only been married a few short months. Our relationship with his mother has only gotten worse.

If only Reuben would stand up to her. Perhaps things would change. But I highly doubt that will ever happen. Even his father walks away when she goes on one of her rampages. I suppose it's easier that way. I must admit I feel sorry for Reuben's *datt*.

My heart melted the other day when he caught my eye momentarily before leaving the kitchen. The deep lines etched on his forehead softened when he looked my way. I swore he mouthed the word *'sorry'* as he passed. It was so quick, I had to take a double look to be sure. Before I could respond, he pulled his straw hat tight on his head and escaped outside. Something I noticed he did often.

Reuben keeps telling me that *Gott* loves his mother as much as he loves me, and I must extend her grace. He assures me that if we give her enough time, she'll calm down and accept things as they are. Besides, there isn't much she can do now that we're married.

Reuben's way of always seeing the good in every situation was one of the reasons I fell in love with him in the first place. But now, after moving to Willow Springs and living so close to his family, his laid-back way of approaching conflict leaves me frustrated.

My family wasn't like this, and I don't understand the dynamics of the Raber household. Maybe it's the cultural differences? I was raised in a more contemporary Mennonite home. And even though my parents were gone a lot on mission trips, religion and values were at the core of our family. My mother respected my father, and I don't remember a time when she voiced her opinions in such a bold manner. And never in front of us children. If they did disagree, it was behind closed doors. Our home was loving and peaceful, except when I pushed the limits. I was a wild child, as my parents often reminded me. Loud and opinionated and always full of words.

When I called to cry on my mother's shoulder from the phone shanty the other day, she kindly reminded me that I often acted much like Saloma does. Nobody likes to have their faults pointed out, and that includes me. I cut my call short and told Reuben that my mother was crazy. Reuben smiled and quickly inserted that perhaps I was frustrated because I saw a little of myself in his mother.

It wasn't that at all. It was that Reuben was too quiet and much too afraid of his mother to stand up for me...his *fraa*. It was the least he could do since I left my home in Sugarcreek so he could stay and help his *bruders* with the farm. I left my church, sister, parents, and community for what? To deal with a heartless mother-in-law who couldn't care less about anything but herself.

Even before we were married, she made it perfectly clear that I wasn't suitable for her son. I thought she would change her mind, especially since I joined the church and agreed to adapt to a more conservative way of Amish life.

As I sit here, feeling sorry for myself, I can't help but remember what my sweet neighbor, Lydia, shared with me just this morning.

"Allie, every family struggles with sin and character flaws. In their own way, they all experience conflict and brokenness. But we must remember that *Gott* intentionally put the members of your family together for a purpose. It's Satan who is determined to break the foundation *Gott* orchestrated. Gott intends you to use those battles to draw closer to Him as Satan wants to use them to tear families apart."

She patted my arm when I rolled my eyes and said, "You have everything you need to find encouragement and hope in the *Gott's* Word. Go to it and meditate on his promises. He'll give you practical steps to heal the brokenness you're experiencing."

It seemed like too much to comprehend, and I let out a long sigh. The thought of trying to work through his mother's bad attitude was a daunting task. How on earth did I think things would change? I saw all the signs beforehand but chose to ignore them for love. I was sure once we were married, Reuben would come to my rescue and cling to me like the Bible says he should. Instead, he walks around on pins and needles and tries to keep peace with me while not upsetting her.

Lydia's words helped, and I pondered her advice most of the day. She offered me truth and clarity, along with some much-needed encouragement.

Perhaps *Gott* did have motivation for placing me in the Raber family. What that might be is a mystery for sure and certain.

All I want is a peaceful and loving home. A husband who will stand by my side in all circumstances and in-laws who consider me a blessing rather than a curse.

"Please, Lord, help me see your goodness in all things. I know your plans are greater than anything I can imagine. Help me love Saloma as you love her. You hand-picked my parents,

sibling, husband, and even mother-in-law. The challenges I'm facing are not a surprise to you, I'm sure of it. It's part of your plan that I might grow in faith and character. Search my heart, oh Lord, show me where I may fall short of your loving grace…amen."

***

With a thundering boom, the back door bounced off its frame as Saloma pushed into Allie's kitchen, dropping a basket of green beans at her feet.

After her heartfelt plea to *Gott*, Allie tried to remain calm. "Help me, Lord," she muttered quietly.

Saloma scoffed. "You'll need more than help from the Lord if you expect to get these canned and the kitchen cleaned before Reuben gets home."

It took every fiber of her being for Allie to keep her mouth from spitting out what her heart revealed. Her mother's words came to mind as she struggled to control her emotions. *"Your reactions will only go where your heart has already gone."*

Allie moved the basket to the table, and before she could offer a polite thank you, Saloma continued. "I suppose you don't know the first thing about putting up vegetables. By the look of your garden, I also suspect your canning skills are lacking."

This shouldn't be this hard, Allie thought. *Just tell her thank you and show her to the door.* Repeating some of her mother's words in her head, she moved the peck of beans to the sink. *Our words reveal the kingdom we are in pursuit of...*

Filling her lungs, she squared her shoulders and faced her mother-in-law. "I'm quite capable of canning green beans." Pausing long enough to take another breath, she asked, "Did these come from your garden?"

"That's a stupid question. Where else would they come from?" Saloma snapped.

As if a swarm of honeybees had entered the kitchen, a humming filled her head and flowed through her veins. She had to remind herself to take long, steady breaths. "Okay, then," she muttered, her gaze never leaving the woman's face. Like showing dominance when training a dog, she refused to avert her eyes from Saloma's glare. Besides, it was her kitchen that Saloma invaded. While she fought to keep her words under control, she wasn't about to let the woman lay claim to her home.

She ushered Saloma to the door without offering the woman a cool drink or a place to sit. "Thank you for the beans. I won't let them go to waste."

Saloma uttered in annoyance, "You best not; it took me an hour to pick them."

Allie moved back to the sink and watched the older woman walk along the path back to Raber's Farm & Produce along Willow Creek. While she loved Reuben's work to restore the *doddi haus*, it sat too close to her in-law's produce business for her liking. Panic knifed through Allie, and the fear that nothing would ever change hurled her back to a state of regret.

Moving to the table, she rested her chin in the palms of her hands, closed her eyes, and tried to escape to those early days when Reuben's undying love for her was all she needed.

Becoming a wife didn't come with an owner's manual, and she received very little wisdom to help her along the way. Oh, she knew what was expected of her according to her culture, but the emotional part of marriage and family dynamics left her weary.

What happens when the message women receive about being meek and mild, ready to serve at all costs and the pressure of being a *Gottly* wife leaves one feeling like a failure?

Suddenly she felt like she would never measure up to Saloma Raber's standards. She would never be good enough to be a Raber. Not kind enough, not gracious enough, not smart enough, not disciplined enough.

How she longed for those carefree months when Reuben and she first fell in love. The days were filled with so much hope and joy about the future. The desire of their hearts was challenged at every turn until they ran away and got married. Had she known then what she knew now, she may have changed her path's direction.

***

Saloma Raber

Why that boy chose to marry her is beyond me. She's too worldly to ever make a good Amish *fraa*. I see problems for sure and certain.

I don't care what Daniel says, she'll never live up to what is expected of her. And that mouth…why I cringe every time she opens it! I could never trust her to work at the produce stand. Lo and behold, she'd offend one of the customers, and we'd be the laughingstock of the *g'may*.

We've worked too hard to become pillars in this community to let one ill-tempered girl spoil our reputation. Besides, people are already questioning Reuben's unexpected marriage. I'm sure people think she's with child. What a disgrace they've brought to our name. And so, help me, if that's the case... I'll just die.

He should have married Virginia Yoder. She would have made a wonderful daughter-in-law. Such a sweet disposition from a good family. She would have made the perfect addition to our business. Her uncle, Levi Yoder's, Strawberry Acres would have complemented our produce farm significantly. How is it I'm the only one who can see that?

But no, Reuben had to go off and get married behind our backs and to a girl from outside our faith. And her parents. Her father is a missionary. Doesn't even own his own home, for goodness' sake, and still rents from the church. How humiliating.

I never dreamed Reuben, out of all my children, would do something so impulsive. As a child, his deliberation and caution often exasperated me. Where did I go wrong with the boy? I should have insisted Daniel talk to Virginia's father sooner. Or better yet, we should have been harder on the boy. Insisted he come into the family business instead of woodworking. Anyone can build furniture. But there are very few produce farms like ours.

And I don't care what Daniel says, I'm not overreacting. Not sure how he can't see what is so evident in front of us. Our son made a foolish choice in choosing Allie Mast as his lifelong mate. Trouble that girl is. Trouble, I say, plain and simple.

Tracy Fredrychowski

CHAPTER 1

Eight Months Earlier

S weat trickled between Reuben Raber's shoulder blades as he swatted a fly from his face. He didn't know what was more annoying; his mother yapping in his ear or the swarm of flies hovering around the full wheelbarrow.

"*Mamm*, like I said, I'll join the church when I feel it's right."

His mother balanced her hands on her hips. "Why do you have to be so stubborn? Your *bruders* wasted no time in taking their kneeling vow by the time they were your age. And look at them now, all settled down, married, and adding a fresh supply of *kinner* to the family."

Reuben threw another shovel of manure in the waiting cart and grinned inwardly when some of it splattered on his mother's apron.

Saloma groaned at her son's carelessness. "Your *datt* is counting on you to help with the farm, and I could use another daughter-in-law to help ease the load in the cider mill come fall."

Reuben had so much to say, but adding fuel to his mother's already burning embers would do nothing but prolong him from finishing his chores. His mother, incapable of a quiet moment, continued. "And don't think for one minute I don't know about you meeting that Mennonite girl from Sugarcreek at *The Book Cellar*. It was all my *schwesters* could talk about at our work frolic yesterday."

Without commenting, he pushed the steaming load onto the compost pile outside. As he walked away, his mother hollered more disapproval, and when he didn't respond, she turned toward the house.

Two days earlier, he had met Allie Mast at the bookstore. For months, they'd been getting to know one another over coffee and chats about some of their favorite authors. She'd rave about her favorite fiction authors, and he'd share stories from his.

He hung the pitchfork and leaned the wheelbarrow against the back wall, slipping around the corner to avoid his mother's path. Then he checked his pocket watch. Only four more hours until his cousin Elwin was due to pick him up, and he still had much to do before his father would allow him to take off for the evening.

The last thing he wanted was to be held up from his date with Allie, even if he had to find a more private place to meet and use Elwin as a cover.

***

Saloma let the door slam as she marched back into the house. In all her thirty years of raising children, Reuben was the only one who stirred her up like yellow jackets burrowing a hole in a rotten apple.

After running herself a glass of water, she plopped down in her chair and mumbled, "If he thinks for one minute, I'll sit back and let him marry outside the *g'may*; he has another think coming. We've worked too hard to make a name for ourselves, and I won't have the likes of that girl from the wrong side of the tracks mothering my grandbabies."

Raber Farms had spanned two generations and was the lifeblood of Willow Springs, selling fresh produce, apples, and cider as far north as Lake Erie and south to Pittsburgh. They employed over fifty employees at the height of the operation and needed each family member to pull their weight. It seemed only Reuben had little interest in the family business, no matter what the cost to his reputation.

She held the cold glass to her forehead, wiped the moisture away from her upper lip with the back of her hand, and thought. *Maybe I'm going about this all wrong. Perhaps a few words with the bishop will put an end to this. Besides, he owes me. I've kept his secret hidden all these years. It's all the leverage I'll need to secure his cooperation...*

***

Reuben followed the sound of his father's hammer and steadied himself on the gate until his father completed his task. Glancing over the glistening bare spot on the top of his father's head, he assured himself his mother had returned to the house before he began.

"I've completed everything you asked me to do. Are you good with me calling it a day?"

Without looking up from the farm implement he was working on; his father grunted a response. "What did you do to get your mother all worked up?"

"Woke up, I suppose."

His father tilted his head and grinned. "Guess I can relate to that one."

"Really, *Datt*, I have no idea what her problem is. I'm sure it has something to do with her *schwesters* gossip and the Amish grapevine at work in my life."

Daniel Raber was a man of few words. He had reconciled to the fact that his wife took the lead in most conversations, giving him little wiggle room to voice his own opinions. When it mattered most, he'd stand his ground, but when it came to Saloma Raber, she often had the last word, and he was okay with that.

She was a good mother, savvy businesswoman, and gave him nine sons with a few of them a spitting image of herself, right down to her boisterous personality.

"Son, you must remember that there is something fierce about your *mamm*. If she feels one of her children is threatened, she will go into defense mode. I'm sure she feels like she needs to protect you somehow."

"I'm twenty-one, and I hardly need guarding. Besides, who or what does she need to protect me from?"

"Not sure; how about you tell me?"

Reuben removed his hat and wiped his forehead with the back of his hand. "I suppose she's all worked up about Allie Mast."

"The young Mennonite girl helping out at Shetler's Grocery?"

"*Jah*. It seems Aunt Melda saw us at the bookstore several times and mentioned it to *Mamm*."

Daniel stood and wiped the grease off the hammer with a red shop rag he pulled from his pocket. "I'm not in the habit of telling any of you boys who you should or shouldn't spend time with, but are you sure that's the best choice?"

Reuben pondered his father's question a moment before responding. "Why should it matter?"

Daniel propped his foot on the plow hitch and rested his elbow on his knee while wiping grease off another tool. "I suspect your *mamm* is worried the girl will keep you from joining the church."

"And what if she does? I've not been baptized, so it's not like I'd be shunned or banned from the family. It's my choice to decide whether to join the Amish church or not."

Reuben watched as his father's jaw quivered slightly, trying to find the right words to respond to his statement.

"*Jah*, it is your decision. It's just that all your *bruders* joined the church. We assumed you'd do the same."

"All I know is even if I do, I would be joining the New Order Fellowship and not the Old Order."

Daniel raised an eyebrow. "You best not say that to your *mamm* just yet. Let her come to terms with you stepping outside our church district first."

"Will you talk to her?"

His father let out a deep-throated groan. "I learned long ago that my job was to plant the seed and then walk away. I've already told her to let it be. If the seed grows into a weed, all I can do is pluck it out before it chokes out the other plants."

Reuben furrowed his eyebrows together, trying to make sense of his father's analogy.

His father stood up and firmly stated, "Look, I'm not watering this plant. I'm praying she'll forget about it, and it will wither away as fast as it took root. I suggest you do the same.

In the meantime, find someplace more private to step out with this girl. No sense in cultivating a field of weeds for everyone to see unless necessary."

As Reuben walked away, something was stirring inside. Almost a sense of bitterness that his mother was dismissing Allie before she had even met her. He'd never been a confrontational young man, nor had he ever been in a fight.

However, suddenly he felt like he was going into battle. He was quiet and thoughtful and felt his strength came from his passivity. He was safe and dependable and knew he could offer Allie a good life. But at that moment, heat surged through his veins, giving him the courage to confront his mother head-on.

When he returned to the house, he felt sure this was one instance when he needed to stand up for what he believed in. Not that Allie was helpless in the least. In fact, the opposite; she was strong and sure of herself like no other girl he'd ever met. But when it came to his mother, he needed to stand his ground, for Allie's sake.

Just the thought of her dark hair and crystal blue eyes fluttered through his mind. While it wasn't in his custom to look at outward beauty as much as the condition of one's heart, he couldn't help but let her beauty draw out his strength. She inspired him to be a hero, especially regarding his overbearing mother. And he was determined to put a stop to his mother's meddling before it took root.

He couldn't take the gamble that his well-meaning mother would come in the middle of his budding relationship with the pretty Allie Mast. He wouldn't stand for it, and it was time he let her know.

***

Rueben rested his hand on the doorknob and hesitated to whisper a prayer before entering his mother's kitchen.

"Lord, help me be patient and loving but firm."

After letting the screen door slam, Reuben took off his hat and stood at the door, waiting for his mother to acknowledge his arrival.

With a quick glance over her shoulder, she spat, "There's no need to let that door bang so hard. After all my yammering about it, I thought you boys would learn to close it softly by now."

When Reuben didn't move or respond, she turned and dried her hands on her apron. "You're stewing about something. Spit it out. I have things to do, and standing here watching you fumble with your attentions isn't one of them."

After clearing his throat, he stated, "I'm stepping out with Allie, and I'd appreciate you keeping your opinions to yourself."

He knew by the color change creeping up her neck, his quest for justice would be risky. Reuben licked his dry lips. "I'm a man, and I'm capable of making my own decisions."

Saloma tossed her head back and snorted out a condemning laugh. "A man? If you were a man, you'd know what division you'll cause in this family if you marry outside your Amish faith. Plus, if you were a man, as you say, you would know that your *datt* and *bruders* need your help in the family business more than chasing your hair-brained idea of being a carpenter. Furniture makers are a dime a dozen."

Reuben shuffled his feet. "I don't remember you voicing your opinion so loudly with the other boys."

"I didn't need to. They found good Amish girls and stayed close by."

"What makes you think Allie couldn't be as good as any of them?"

"She's been exposed to the world, that's why. There is no way she could give all that up."

"You don't even know her. How can you judge someone you've never even spoken to?"

Saloma moved to the stove to check on dinner. "I've talked to her plenty of times at Shetler's."

"About what? The weather?"

"It doesn't matter what we've talked about. What matters is a mother knows these things, and that girl would never fit into our world."

Reuben's legs became wobbly, and his jaw tightened at her comment. "She doesn't need to fit into your world; she needs to fit into mine."

"I forbid it," Saloma demanded. "There is no way I'll permit you to go further with that girl. Besides, she can't be much more than sixteen. You might as well set your sight on someone else because I'll never give you my blessing."

Her voice said quite clearly that their talk was over, and he was dismissed, but Reuben was set on not allowing his mother to have the last word this time.

In a brave move, he walked closer to his mother's side, held her elbow firmly, and whispered in a low husky voice, "Don't push me on this, *Mamm*. You won't win this one."

Saloma grimaced. "I wouldn't be so sure about that."

Before leaving her side, he moved closer, with the light of battle in his eyes. "This is my life, not yours, and you'll have no say in who I choose to spend my time with."

"Out of the question. I mean it. No is no. It will never work. You are just asking for heartache with that one. Too many obstacles to overcome."

A fresh adrenaline rush surged around his heart, and he grunted a deep sigh as he walked outside, letting the door slam louder than before.

***

Saloma pushed a stray hair off her forehead and sank to a kitchen chair. Reuben had never stood his ground before, which caught her off guard. Out of all her boys, Reuben was always the one to follow the rules. This was a side of him she'd never seen before, and if she was honest with herself, she didn't much like it. How dare he go against her so forcefully? The whole

24

scene left her wondering if there was more to his relationship with the girl than she thought.

Pulling herself together, she turned off the stove before leaving to find her husband. Someone needed to have a word with the boy for sure and certain.

She shielded her eyes from the late afternoon sun and watched Reuben's form disappear over the ridge in the yard leading to the road. The thought of him storming off, most likely to meet Allie, infuriated her even more. Pulling her sweater tight to ward off an early fall cold spell, she headed to the backfield, where Daniel picked apples.

It didn't take her but a few minutes to locate Daniel in a cluster of gala apple trees. The bucket he had strapped in front of him was overflowing and needed to be emptied. She pushed the apple cart toward him, and he smiled at her thoughtfulness.

"By the look on your face, I assume this isn't a friendly visit."

Saloma positioned her hands on her hips. "I just don't know what to make of that boy."

"While we have nine boys, do you want to tell me which one you are referring to?"

"You know good and well which one. Reuben."

She sighed before continuing. "Do you know he had the nerve to walk into my kitchen and tell me to keep my opinions to myself?"

Daniel snickered. "Got a little backbone, did he?"

"Backbone? I call it being disrespectful. I know we raised him better than the way he just spoke to me."

"Now, Saloma, I'm sure you egged him on a bit."

"Whose side are you on? You know as well as I do, the boy isn't making much sense."

Daniel positioned the straps to the bucket over his shoulders and started picking apples as Saloma followed him into the trees. "I never dreamed it would be Reuben we had to worry about. He was always such a polite and dutiful boy. Never gave me any worry that he wouldn't join the church and settle down close by."

Daniel dropped a few apples in the empty bucket. "Could it be he's your last, and you're not ready to let him go?"

"He can go all he wants."

Daniel lifted his chin in her direction. "As long as it coincides with the path you envisioned?"

She stammered, "Well, no...not just so."

"Then what is it? Why are you so set against this girl?"

"I'm not sure. Call it mother's intuition. But there is something about the girl that doesn't sit right with me."

"But you've not even given her a chance."

Saloma crossed her arms across her body. "Right now, this discussion isn't about her as much as it's about how he spoke to me. What are you going to do about that?"

The longer it took for him to answer, the more agitated she became. "So? What are you going to do?"

"Nothing."

"Nothing? What do you mean nothing?"

"The boy is not doing anything that the other boys didn't do. He's branching out to the other side of boyhood and becoming a man. The last person he needs telling him how to run his life is his *mamm*."

"That's the craziest thing I've ever heard you say. The other boys didn't give me pushback like this."

"Yes, they did. You just don't remember because they did it to me, not you. Reuben has always been closer to you, and that's why it's affecting you so. Trust me. His desire for independence will force him to briefly push you out of his life, but he'll be back. I promise."

27

She turned and stormed off, yelling over her shoulder, "Your logic isn't helping. It's making me more frustrated."

As Saloma walked to the house, a million thoughts were whirling through her head. *If Daniel wouldn't help, she'd go to someone who would. Bishop Weaver owed her, and she was determined to convince him to help her. Plus, she needed to invite Virginia Yoder to dinner. Maybe if Reuben spent more time with Virginia, he'd see how perfectly they got along. Besides, what boy doesn't want his fraa to get along with his mother?*

CHAPTER 2

Allie Mast's eyes snapped open, but she lay still, trying to make sense of the dream that awoke her. Two lions? Reuben? A river? She shook her head, trying to force the image away. When nothing made sense, she pushed the covers aside and sat on the edge of her bed to stretch that last remnant of sleep from her body. After completing preparations for the day, she headed to the window to welcome the first peeks of the sun.

A few subtle threads of mist slipped through the yellowing maple trees surrounding the small house behind Shetler's Grocery. Allie quickly slipped on a work dress, donned a sweater to ward off the early morning chill, and grabbed her shoes.

Mornings alongside Willow Creek were her favorite time of the day. Her shift at the grocery wasn't due to start for another two hours, which gave her plenty of time to grab breakfast and head to the creek.

She never dreamed she would have loved working at Shetler's as much as she had. When her mother's sister offered her a job, she quickly accepted the position and moved the two hours east to Willow Springs. Barely seventeen, she enjoyed her newfound independence, even under the watchful eye of her uncle's aging mother, Sylvia Shetler, who lived with her in the tiny *doddi haus*.

Life couldn't be more perfect, especially after meeting Reuben Raber. Just the thought of how he always smelled of wood shavings and how the little stubble on his chin turned so dark by evening made her tingle with excitement. She pondered all the things she loved about him while she tucked a banana muffin in her pocket and headed out the door.

His quiet manner, the way he thought long about everything before answering, but most of all, they shared a love for the written word. At home in Sugarcreek, she had to hide her books and only read late at night. But with Reuben, they spent countless hours at the bookstore comparing notes about characters and storylines. Most of the time, they just sat sipping their coffee and saying nothing. She was sure their comfort and ease with each other was meant to be.

They did have a few differences that they would need to work through, but it was something that could be discussed and decided upon. One was the difference in their churches. Allie came from a contemporary Mennonite background where cars and cell phones were allowed. Even though the dress code was still much like Reuben's community, her dresses were much brighter, and she was allowed to wear prints, as Reuben's family still followed the Old Order way of life that prohibited such sophisticated colors and fabrics.

While still pulled up, her hair was covered with a small circular lace covering. It wasn't uncommon for the girls to wear prettier shoes rather than the typical black-soled ones she noticed some Amish girls in the area wearing.

While her upbringing was similar to Reuben's, in many ways, it was different. Whereas Reuben's father concentrated on building his business and was quite wealthy as far as she could tell, her father was a prison minister and spent all his spare time and money evangelizing to the broken men of the world.

They definitely had obstacles to overcome, and she prayed they could find a way to make their union work...for both their families.

The morning air was crisp, and she took a deep breath and held her face to the rising sun. Its rays feathered her face, and she closed her eyes and remembered the first time she had seen Reuben.

It had been outside the *Book Cellar.* He stood with his foot up on the bench to the right of the door, talking to a small group of boys. As she walked by, he tipped his straw hat, and her heart did a little flip. There was something about him that made her take a seat next to the window inside so she could steal a closer look. He had robust, chiseled features, his jaw softened when he smiled, and he had a seriousness about him that she found appealing. He wasn't loud or obnoxious like a few of the other young men. But he stood quiet, just observing as if he was deep in thought.

That day, he had sunglasses on, so she couldn't see the color of his eyes, but she imagined they were a mysterious gray blue, like the sky right before a storm rolled in. To her pleasant surprise, she'd guessed correctly when he stepped inside and revealed his eyes.

It was a warm day the first time she noticed him; his dark hair lay plastered to his forehead beneath his hat. He wore his sleeves rolled up, revealing just a hint of manual labor beneath the taut light blue fabric. And those shoulders. She'd always been attracted to strong shoulders. Ones that could bear the weight of the world if he had to.

"Heavens, I think I've been reading one too many romance books," she whispered as she fanned her flushed face and shook the memory from her mind.

She brushed a few leaves from the fallen log near the creek, positioned herself so the sun could warm her, and opened her book.

She paused long enough to look to the end of the path where it intersected with the paved road and smiled. She'd walk to the road in twelve hours, and Reuben and Elwin would pick her up for their planned coffee date.

His cousin Elwin was a funny one. He was always up for a good laugh, not a serious bone in his body, and acted more like a twelve-year-old than nineteen.

At first, she was curious to know why he tagged along with us everywhere they went. Rueben explained that he would feel better if they kept their dates to public places and always had a chaperone so nothing would get back to her parents that would make them think he wasn't worthy of her attention. What a gentleman to always put her reputation first and foremost in his mind. She fell in love with him even more that day.

Now, she'd be lying to herself if she didn't admit she wouldn't mind him holding her hand occasionally. But she understood their *g'may* enforced a no-touching rule until marriage. Her Sugarcreek community wasn't so strict, and she'd stepped out with a boy who stole a kiss or two and always took her hand when they were alone. But again, respecting her honor was so appealing. It was like Reuben was her knight in shining armor, as her latest read referred to the hero.

She closed her book and decided reading wouldn't happen, so she picked up a rock and headed to the creek. Restless, she wondered if Reuben could break out of their routine and go for a walk instead. They could take their coffee and stroll around town. He was so predictable that she hoped she could get him to do something unexpected. Besides, how much more public would it be than a stroll through downtown Willow Springs?

As she released the flat stone and let it soar across the water's edge like Reuben taught her, she couldn't help but remember how unusually quiet he was last week. When they picked her up, he barely said hello until they had settled into their regular table at the *Book Cellar*. Elwin left to meet a few friends at the *Restaurant on the Corner* and said he'd return at nine.

For some reason, Reuben, as soon as he delivered their regular coffee drinks, her a vanilla lavender latte and him a black coffee with extra honey, lost himself in his current read. She tried to engage him in dialogue, but his one-word answers shut her out until she stopped trying. Something was bothering him; she was sure of it. The one comment he made was about his mother, which was short and didn't make any sense without further explanation.

She rubbed her eyes and tried to remember what he had said. Something about his mother thinking the sun rose just to hear her crow. It didn't make sense then, and it surely doesn't make sense now.

Allie didn't know much about Saloma Raber other than what Sylvia told her when she asked about her. Her warning didn't pinpoint anything specific, but it made her take notice of the tone Sylvia used.

"Be careful with that one." The old woman's mouth turned briefly into a curl of concern, but she wouldn't say another word and went back to working on the crocheted Afghan she held in her lap.

After that evening, Allie wondered if Reuben, being a man of too few words and her erring on the side of too many, would cause friction between them. It was the first time in the three months that she questioned whether their personality differences would be an issue. It wasn't so much right or wrong; she liked to be forthright and solve a problem before it got out of hand. Reuben, on the other hand, was more laid back and pondered an issue for days, sometimes weeks, before he voiced a solution.

When she mentioned her concern to Sylvia, she quickly offered her some sound advice.

"Child, you're not nearly old enough to understand all it takes to make a relationship work, but some of the worst conflicts come from being too quick to judge others before we examine our own shortcomings."

She remembered Sylvia delayed a few minutes before she continued with an even more profound point that she wouldn't soon forget.

"It's not important to figure out whose way is better or who is at fault, but rather that the Lord wants us to deal with our own issues first. He chooses us to pray to Him for our eyes to be opened to our own sin before we criticize someone else."

Allie went as far as to write the old woman's comments in her journal that night, hoping she would remember her wise guidance.

***

Allie released the last stone from her hand and gathered her book to head to work. She stopped long enough to watch a cluster of red and orange maple leaves tumble to the ground.

Maybe she'd read one too many romance novels to understand what being in love really meant. But she did know was she was on a journey of the heart. A journey toward womanhood. It was about discovering who she was in Christ and as Reuben's girlfriend. Reuben made it perfectly clear he had plans for their future, and she couldn't stop daydreaming about what that might mean.

At the core, she was a woman who wanted to be loved and to love. She wanted motherhood and a family life, but also to be romanced and have adventure. More than anything, she wanted to be the woman *Gott* had planned her to be, and she prayed that Reuben was the one *Gott* handpicked just for her.

***

It had been a week since Reuben stormed into Saloma's kitchen, and the days that followed left the air between them heavy like the morning dew. Saloma sat on the front porch peeling a basket of apples when she noticed Reuben across the yard hitching up the wagon to go to work.

She wrapped her fingers tightly around an apple and thought. *I need to make time to visit the bishop. He must agree to help me keep Reuben from making the biggest mistake of his life. I know he'll want me to address the issue with Daniel first. Lord knows that didn't get me anywhere. Besides, Daniel has enough to worry about right now with dwindling profits. This is the last thing he needs.*

Dread crept up her chest, and she breathed a long sigh as she pondered. *Why can't the boy see we need him here more than ever? He's being downright selfish, for sure and certain.*

As Reuben drove away without so much as a wave in her direction, she stood and carried her bowl of apples to the kitchen. After covering them with a splash of lemon juice and water, she set them aside and headed to the door, mumbling. "No time like the present."

***

There was something odd about the way Mose Weaver greeted Saloma. It took him a few minutes to acknowledge her as she stood just inside the barn and even longer to understand why she was bothering him with such things. It was like he had lost all comprehension of their shared history and the secret they held tightly. When he laughed and dismissed her concerns, she balanced her hands on her hips and spat, "I can't believe you won't help me with this."

Mose leaned on his pitchfork. "The boy has the right to make his own decisions, and until he joins the church, there really isn't anything I can do. Besides, I doubt he'll join our *g'may*. Most young people are moving toward Bishop Schrock's New Order."

Saloma glanced over her shoulder quickly and moved a couple of steps closer. "You know how hard it is on a family when one wanders from the fold."

She knew she'd hit a nerve when the muscle in his jaw quivered, and he growled. "Thirty years is a long time to hold such things over one's head. You best leave the past where it belongs if you know what's good for you."

She squared her shoulders and stood firm. "*Ach.* Did I hit a tender spot? I bet there would be more than one church member who would be interested in what I know."

Mose drove the tines of the fork in a pile of manure and heaved it over her shoulder to a waiting cart. "Perhaps so. But you know as well as I do that such things are forbidden to be discussed. And I'm sure Daniel would find the part you played in all of it interesting."

Saloma glared into his weather-beaten face and thought. *Threats or no threats, he had more to lose.* However, she couldn't help but wonder what he thought he could do about it. He was the one with the secret. She only discovered it by mistake but knew well enough to tuck the information away for safekeeping until the time was right.

Mose pulled a small leather-bound notebook from his back pocket and held it up. "Don't push too hard, Saloma. You fail to remember that I see and know all around here, and I'm not the only one with skeletons in the cupboards."

"Don't bully me with such things." Saloma struggled to keep her composure. "My life is an open book, and I have nothing to be concerned with. Whatever you think you have on me is surely a stem of lies fabricated to justify your own behavior for sure and certain."

"Are you sure about that?" he asked sarcastically.

The way his eyebrows shifted left her with a gnawing desire to know what was in the journal and how she could get her hands on it. Whatever it was, it would take more than a few weightless threats to keep her from getting what she wanted.

Mose continued to clean out the stall and stated, "If you think for one minute, I'll cave to your ridiculous request, you're crazier than I thought. Leave the lad alone and let him live his own life. Nothing good will come for you or him if you continue to meddle in his affairs."

He paused long enough to catch his breath and continued. "Didn't you learn anything about putting your nose where it doesn't belong thirty years ago?"

"Hence why I'm here," she said with cynicism. She tapped her forefinger on the side of her temple. "I've been keeping those secrets secured in here until I had cause to use them to my advantage."

His laugh rumbled. "Saloma Raber, I'd watch yourself if I were you. Your words display the true condition of your heart. One of these days, you're going to find yourself in a situation you're not going to be able to wiggle yourself out of."

Salona countered with more assertion. "And you can count on the secrets you've kept buried all these years are making their way to the surface." She moved in closer. "All I'm asking is for you to talk to Reuben and convince him to give up this crazy notion of seeing that girl. Her kind will only bring trouble." She lingered in his space. "You, out of anyone should know that best."

His breath landed on her cheek and a firm hand on her arm made a nervous giggle escape her lips.

"This is no laughing manner. You best keep that tongue of yours from wagging or you'll be the one to suffer the consequence not me."

It was his tone that shook her more than his words as she pulled from his grip. She'd leave it now until she had time to rethink her strategy.

Before she could turn to leave, his *fraa* Catherine appeared with a mug of coffee and a plate of cookies.

"Saloma? Had I known you were visiting, I would have brought more. Mose loves warm cookies, so I decided to bring him a treat. Give me a minute, and I'll go fetch more."

"I can't stay. I just stopped by to ask Mose a question. Seems like I got my answer, so I best be going."

"Are you sure you don't have time for a short visit? Brewing a fresh pot of coffee won't take a few minutes."

Saloma turned her back to Catherine and scowled at Mose. "I'm sure."

"Well, maybe next time, *Jah?*"

Saloma walked past her. "I'll make a point to stay longer next time."

A timely breeze created a flurry of freshly fallen leaves that swirled around her ankles like an unseasonable snowstorm as she marched away. A surge of determination overcame her as she toyed with a way to get her hands on the notebook.

At one time, she had been best friends with Catherine. Perhaps it was time to rekindle that old friendship. Maybe then she could find a way to get her hands on his precious notebook.

***

Reuben paused until he was far away from his parent's farm before encouraging his buggy horse to pick up speed. If he didn't hurry, he'd miss meeting Allie before they both had to go to work. Between his job at Byler's Furniture Shop and helping at his family's apple orchard, he didn't have time for much else. But that morning, they planned to meet for a quick coffee before starting their day.

For as long as he could remember, he knew his roots weren't as strong as his *bruders'* when it came to staying Amish. It was becoming clearer and clearer that if he wanted to break free from his mother's ruling thumb, he'd have to break away from his Old Order upbringing.

And if he knew his mother, she was already trying to find a way to stop that from happening. He'd have to quickly step up his arrangements before his mother did something he couldn't dig his way out of.

He said a little prayer that Allie would be open to his proposal. He might not want to remain Amish, but he had enough sense to know he'd have to find a reliable way to support them first. He patted the letter he'd tucked in his pocket from his uncle and thought, it couldn't have come at a better time.

***

Allie paced on the front porch, praying Reuben would get there before her aunt and uncle left to walk to the store. While they didn't object to her seeing Reuben, they wouldn't be happy to know she was meeting with him so early in the day. But no matter how hard she tried not to rush things, all she wanted to do was spend time with Reuben, no matter the cost.

She sat on the front step, pulled her paisley print dress over her knees, and brushed a speck of dirt off her white canvas sneakers. When he pulled into the driveway, she wasted no time running down the steps to meet him. Her heart melted when he hollered, "Wait!" He set the brake and stepped out of the buggy to help her.

Once he joined her inside, he reached over and pulled her closer. Her pulse quickened with his closeness as she leaned onto his shoulder, taking in his masculine scent, she thought. *Indeed, this is who Gott intended me to marry.*

***

Daniel stepped onto the porch and sat next to Saloma on the swing. He barely set it in motion when she snapped, "I don't like this. Not one bit."

He sighed. "What now?"

"Your son, that's what now."

"Oh, let the boy be."

Saloma raised her voice. "Let him be! What, so he can run off and marry that Mennonite girl?"

Daniel let a few seconds of silence fall between them before he continued. "And would that be so bad?" He reached for her hand. "If I remember right, your parents didn't think too highly of me, and we turned out okay."

She snatched her hand away. "That's different; we belonged to the same church."

Daniel smirked. "You really need to let it go."

Saloma planted both feet firmly on the floor, forcing the swing to stop moving. "It's time you did something about it instead of letting me do it all."

If he knew one thing about his *fraa*, it was to not add fuel to an already smoldering fire. Still, he had just enough of her constant badgering about this topic. "Alright, out with it. What do you expect me to do about it?"

"Your *bruder* John sent a letter inviting Reuben to come to Pinecraft to help him with a big furniture order. I expect you to insist he go to Florida tomorrow with Elwin when he makes the apple delivery. It's high time he set his sights on something different. A few weeks in Pinecraft may be the answer."

***

Allie held her hand to her chest. "Oh my, Reuben, yes! This is the best day ever." She hesitated long enough to imprint the moment in her memory. "When?"

Reuben stiffened his shoulders. "That's the issue I need to explain to you."

Allie rested her hand on his arm. She sensed him relaxing under her touch. "There is nothing we can't handle if we do it together."

He snorted. "You haven't met my mother."

She moved in closer. "I'm not worried. And besides, I've met her at the grocery."

"You should be."

"Oh, she doesn't seem that bad."

***

They ran out of time before Reuben could fully enlighten her about his mother. Still, he promised to do so the following evening.

Once her shift started, it was all she could do to wipe the smile from her face. She had promised Reuben she would only breathe a word of his proposal once he had time to talk to her further. So, all she could do was treasure how his voice was like a warm breeze as he declared his love for her and continued to smile the secret away.

It took her co-worker and new friend Virginia Yoder elbowing her to stop daydreaming long enough to wait on the next customer to break Reuben's spell. She stumbled on a greeting. "I'm sorry. What can I get for you?"

Allie tallied the order and slid the brown paper sack across the counter. "Thank you and come again."

Virginia butted shoulders with her and asked, "Are you going to tell me what's got you all girly-eyed this morning, or am I going to have to guess?"

Allie absorbed her question in silence but glanced around the store before whispering, "The young man I've been seeing asked me a very important question this morning."

Allie took notice of the fall of Virginia's chin. Just yesterday, the girl shared that the boy she'd been sweet on for the last four years was interested in another. "I'm sorry. I didn't mean to upset you."

"Don't be silly. There's no reason I can't be happy for you, even if my dreams faded. Maybe watching you will give me new hope for the future. Besides, his mother has invited me to dinner. She thinks if he sees how well we get along, he might change his mind about me."

"Now that's promising." Allie said, "Things happen as they are meant to happen with no splendid plan on our part. *Gott* will do what He wants to do when He wants to."

Virginia smiled. "Sometimes *Gott's* truth is nice to hear. A lot of the time, actually. I just need to remember the Lord may have someone much better planned for me than I can see with my own two eyes or through my own understanding."

Allie gave her a long, understanding look. "He does, I'm certain of it." Allie didn't know why that comforted her, but what she said seemed to help.

Virginia took a breath and spoke softly to hide her pain. "Thanks for reminding me."

Allie took her hand. "So, are you going to go to dinner?"

"I told her I'd think about it and let her know. I'm still not convinced I should pursue him any further. He made it clear there was no hope for a future together."

CHAPTER 3

S aloma's plan was coming together. Virginia had accepted her dinner invitation, Daniel agreed to send Reuben to Florida with Elwin, and if she had her way, Virginia would be going with them. There was more than one way to skim honey from a hive, and she was the master of splitting a hive in two when it became too crowded.

Daniel busted through the door swinging his arm around his face. "Dag nab it, Saloma, I told you to get in touch with Jeramiah Hersberger to get him over here to split those honeybee hives. They must be ready to swarm. They're meaner than my old man's hogs."

"I sent a message to him, but his grandfather said he's out of town and isn't due back for a few weeks."

His frank request startled her, yet oddly, she felt brave enough to share her plans for the evening.

"I've invited Virginia Yoder to dinner."

"Now why on earth would you do that?"

She chewed her bottom lip and wondered if she should tell him more. "I spoke to her mother, and she mentioned that Virginia had been wanting to go visit her grandparents in Pinecraft. I offered her a ride with Reuben and Elwin tomorrow, so I invited her to dinner so they could make plans."

"So, you invited Elwin too?"

"Heaven's no. You know I don't allow that boy in the house, regardless of if he's your *schwester's* boy or not. Until he gets rid of the truck and comes to his senses, he won't set foot under my table."

Daniel shook his head and ran himself a cold glass of water. "All you're doing is pushing the boy further away. I told you to let it be."

"There's no harm in her taking a ride with them."

"What happened to you being put out that he was spending time with Elwin? The last I knew; you forbid him from associating with him."

When she failed to find a believable explanation, he intensified, "I suppose it's okay since it benefits you." He paused for a moment and then lifted his hand, palm out. "I'm not here to pass judgement, but woman, you need to set up camp in one place and stay there. This going back and forth as it serves you drives me crazy."

Saloma took a breath and cut her gaze away from him. "This is an unusual circumstance and called for an unscrupulous plan."

He growled, "Unscrupulous? It's downright deceitful. You bet my words this stunt is going to come back and sting you harder than a swarm of ground bees."

She tried to calm him by grabbing his hand. "Now, Daniel, when have I ever led this family astray? I have a good sense about such things."

She leaned in and kissed his cheek. "Virginia Yoder would make a great addition to our family. You watch and see. Reuben will come to his senses, and if he doesn't tonight, he has three weeks to spend with her in Florida to get his priorities straight."

"You're playing with fire," he warned.

The tension they'd been holding inside released just a little, and she felt confident she could respond. "I like to think I'm the type of mother who would put herself at risk for the betterment of her family."

He pulled his hat over his forehead. "It's more like you're dumping gasoline on a grass fire. Let's hope you never have to be the one to put it out yourself."

"*Jah*, Daniel. You worry too much. You manage the farm and let me tend to these *kinner*."

"*Kinner*? You only got one left in the *haus*, and he's about to fly the coop with your endless interfering."

***

The screech of the metal door gliding along its track alerted Daniel to his son's arrival home. All afternoon, he contemplated whether he needed to soften the blow and alert Reuben to his mother's plan or let it all come to a head at dinner. He chose the first, hoping to spare Virginia the embarrassment of a family argument.

He tapped his pipe on the back of his hand and refilled it with fresh tobacco as Reuben unhitched the buggy and moved it inside. Balancing the shank between his teeth and cupping the chamber, he lit it, allowing a circle of smoke to encase his head as he waited for the boy to return to the horse.

Daniel led their buggy horse to the stalls, certain Reuben would soon follow.

The two worked seamlessly to remove the harness, rub the black Standardbred down, and fill the water and grain buckets. Once the horse was comfortable, Daniel took a seat on an overturned bucket and pointed for Reuben to join him.

"Something on your mind, *Datt*?"

"Your *mamm* said my *bruder* John has some work for you at his furniture shop?"

Reuben took out the letter. "*Jah*, he says one of his workers got hurt, and he's in a bind with a big order." Reuben paused to re-read the letter briefly. "Seems good woodcrafters are hard to find in Florida. Nobody wants to work, or they don't have the skills required for the quality of work Uncle John expects."

"Is that something you're interested in helping him with?"

"*Jah*, I think so."

I could use the extra cash, and now that I'm twenty-one and don't need to pass on my pay to you and *Mamm*, I think it would be wise to build up my bank account."

"Are you saving for anything specific?"

Daniel knew good and well precisely what the boy was planning, but he wanted to hear it for himself. Any young man stepping out with a young girl had the same thing in mind. One, to find a steady job to support a family, and two, to have enough money set aside to set up a house somewhere. Both things weighed heavily on a man's mind when it came time to settle down.

***

Reuben looked over at his *datt*. He was never good at awkward banter and wasn't sure how honest he could be. He wondered if his *mamm* had soured him to the idea of Allie Mast. And if so, he wasn't in any mood to get into it. After Allie's quick yes that morning, his brain raced with ideas on how they could get married without his mother sabotaging their plans before they were even made.

He reached down, picked up a piece of straw from the floor, and twirled it between his fingers. "Life is complicated, ain't so?"

"It can be," Daniel said, with a sense of curiosity in his tone.

Reuben was burningly curious about what his father really thought of his situation and wondered if he dared ask. He hesitated a few moments, hoping the silence would give him enough courage to inquire. "*Mamm* had once said that *Doddi* Raber didn't think you should marry her. Is that correct?"

His father's long, graying beard moved slightly when he laughed. "*Jah*. He didn't much like your mother. Said she was too bossy, and a house could only have one manager."

"But you married her anyways? Didn't that cause issues with you and your parents?"

Daniel took a long draw on his pipe and asked, "You think that might be the case with Allie Mast?"

"I'm afraid so."

His father balanced his elbow on his knee and looked at him, taking on a sense of seriousness. "I suspect you're right even though I don't agree with your mother's tactics. I must let you in on something before we go in for dinner."

"Not so sure I'm going to like what you have to say just by your tone."

"I'm sure you're not. But before I get into that, know that I have Elwin taking a load of apples to Sarasota early tomorrow morning. Since John needs you right away, you can go with him to save the cost of a bus ticket."

"Tomorrow? I hadn't thought I would leave so quickly. There are some things I need to take care of first."

"Whatever it is, you can take care of them when you return. There is no sense in wasting money when you can tag along with your cousin."

His father sent him a warning look, as if to say there was no use in arguing about it. Warming up to the idea of saving money, he conceded that it was the best plan. For most of his life, he kept his views and feelings to himself, but in the last few months, he felt himself getting braver in voicing his opinions.

"I suppose I should take advantage of the free ride. But can't we leave a little later so I can take care of at least one thing before I take off?"

His father shook his head. "I hear a hurricane is blowing in from the Gulf of Mexico and is due to make landfall in three days near Tampa. I want Elwin gone and back before the storm hits. The only way to do that is to leave bright and early tomorrow morning."

Reuben rubbed his jaw, relieving the itch of a day's worth of stubble. "Wouldn't it be wiser to wait until after the storm passes?"

"Best get that delivery made beforehand. Never know what the roads will be like afterward."

Reuben knew when he was defeated and stood. "I guess."

"Son, sit back down. That's not all."

Something about how his father looked at him alerted him to something dreadful.

"Virginia Yoder is here."

The creases on Reuben's forehead deepened. "What for?"

"Your *mamm* invited her to dinner. Seems her *grossmommi* lives in Pinecraft, and she wants to go for a visit. Your mother offered her a ride with Elwin since he's going that way."

Reuben seethed. Heat boiled through his veins at the thought of his mother's conniving manner. "How could she? If she thinks for one minute, I don't know what she's doing, she's crazy."

"Now, boy, calm down. She means well. Besides, it's just a ride. No harm in that."

"But *Datt*, you know what she's trying to do. She's been harping on and on about Virginia Yoder for months now. She's a sweet girl, but not for me."

His father stood and carried both buckets to the side of the barn. "Let's just get through dinner without making the girl uncomfortable, and we can deal with your mother another time. I think she will stay in your *bruder's* old room tonight so you can get on the road before daybreak."

Reuben turned away to hide his frustration. There was no doubt that the battle with his mother was just beginning. She may have won this round, but he was determined not to let history repeat itself.

***

The air around the supper table was sickeningly sweet, even more so than the honey his mother drizzled over the biscuits as she placed them on the table. To little avail, she tried to pull Reuben into the chit-chat in the most innocent way.

After the silent prayer, in which Reuben had to fight the judgments of his head from turning ugly, his mother asked,

"Have you seen the wonderful quilt Virginia has on display in the Quilt Market's front window?"

With an edge to his tone, he said, "What makes you think I have time to take in such things?"

His father threw him a disapproving glare, and he offered a rebuttal. "I'm sure it's beautiful. I'll look at it the next time I'm in town."

Virginia cleared her throat and softly asked, "Is there anything specific you're working on at Byler's? I stopped by the other day with my mother, and we were admiring the fine pieces in the showroom."

A wave of guilt settled in, and he softened his stance. It wasn't Virginia's fault that his mother had overstepped boundaries. The poor girl, as always, had a calming manner about her. To be exact, it was one of the reasons he chose to break it off with her. Their personalities were too similar, and he feared they wouldn't challenge each other enough to make a lasting relationship. As he listened to her observation of some of the pieces he contributed to the showroom, he couldn't help but remember Elwin's comment after learning he had broken it off with her.

"You'll be much happier with a woman more like your mamm than yourself. You need someone to light a fire under you occasionally...if you know what I mean."

At the time, he didn't know what he meant, but he understood once he met Allie. Allie had a spark about her. She wasn't afraid to speak her mind. He never had to worry about what to say or think when Allie was around.

He smiled and nodded as Virginia engaged in a deeper discussion with his mother, which gave him ample time to devise a plan to let Allie know of his travel plans.

"Reuben! Virginia asked you a question."

He glanced at her, and the poor thing looked flustered by his mother's terse nature. "I'm sorry. I guess I wasn't listening."

"That's okay. I was just asking how long you think you might stay in Pinecraft?"

"At least a few weeks. Looks like Uncle John has a good bit of work to get out."

"Have you ever been to Florida this time of year?"

"Nope. Never been there at all."

Virginia offered him a bashful smile and then continued. "Well, it's downright delightful this time of the year. There's a lull in late fall, right before the snowbirds start arriving, that prepares the locals for the upcoming winter season.

Everyone is buzzing about who will stay the winter and who will only come for a short visit. Gardens are freshened up, porches and lawn furniture are washed and displayed in cozy little conversation groupings, and Pinecraft Park is spruced up in anticipation of evening *singeons* and shuffleboard."

"Sounds like a busy time."

"It is. I can't wait." Virginia tipped her head back, folded her hands under her chin, and continued. "There is a define sweet saltiness that blows in from the ocean that can't be matched anywhere else I've ever been." She leaned further into the table. "And let me tell you about the Coffee Café. They have the best specialty drinks around. They are literally to die for! It's the perfect day when I can grab a morning coffee and then return at night to go across the street to the Ice Cream Shoppe for soft serve. Absolutely heavenly."

He couldn't help but smile at her enthusiasm. "You do love your ice cream," he replied.

Saloma started to clear the table. "Sounds like you know all the best spots. Perhaps you can play tour guide and show Reuben all Sarasota has to offer."

He quickly stated, "I'll not have much time for socializing. I'm not going on vacation; I'm going to work."

Virginia stood and carried a bowl to the counter. "All work and no play is boring. I look forward to my yearly trip. It's the one time I get to have some fun. They have a saying in Pinecraft, "'What happens in Pinecraft stays in Pinecraft.'"

Reuben lifted one eyebrow and snarled, "That sounds dangerous."

Her lips softened into a smile that became a laugh. "No danger of that. I don't do anything in Florida I wouldn't do right here in Willow Springs. Well, except go swimming." She took the glass out of his hand before he could set it down and continued. "Wait until you see the Siesta Key. The water is so blue, and the sand is so white it looks like a painting."

The thought of seeing the ocean did sound appealing, but he wouldn't let Virginia know that. For some odd reason, he felt guilty for even thinking of enjoying such things without Allie. *That's right, Allie,* he thought. *I need to let her know what's going on.* Before he had a chance to excuse himself, his mother demanded he take Virginia to the front porch to watch the sunset over the apple orchard.

"This time of day has the most beautiful sky display." His mother guided Virginia to the door and scowled back at Reuben to follow her.

"If you think *Gott* paints a picture over the ocean, you haven't seen anything until you witness the sun fall behind the apple trees on the Raber farm."

Reuben had to agree with his mother, even though he didn't appreciate her tactics to get them alone. Once on the porch, he sat in one of the hickory rockers, and Virginia claimed the other. His mother pushed the screen door open and waved her hand toward the swing. "Now, that won't do. Reuben, you know the best view is from the swing."

The muscles in Reuben's shoulders tensed as he followed Virginia to the swing. In one swift glance, he threw his mother a disapproving scowl. She didn't respond but waved him on and retreated to the kitchen.

Without a word, they watched as the evening sky gathered an abundant array of orange and red as a backdrop to the yellowing apple trees. The fields anchoring the manicured trees brimmed with goldenrod and butterfly weed. In one quick swoop, an evening owl glided across the meadow already on the hunt.

Reuben pointed. "Did you see that?"

"I wonder what he's looking for."

"An evening snack, I'm sure."

Virginia crossed her legs and pulled her sweater in tight. "Your mother was right. It is beautiful here. I can almost smell the apples in the air."

"I think what you're smelling is cider. I think my *bruders* are pressing apples already."

"Where do they do that?"

He stood and pointed over the landscape to the building silhouetted against the sky. "Over there is where we wash the apples, then press and bottle the cider."

"We? Have you changed your mind about working with your *datt* and *bruders*? I thought you didn't have any interest in farming?"

"No, I haven't changed my mind. But I do help when I have time."

He walked back to the swing and sat next to her. For only a moment, he scanned her features. She glanced back, and the soft smile on her face did a strange thing to his insides.

Suddenly, sitting on the porch with her seemed wrong. All he could envision was what Allie would think if she saw how close they sat. Abruptly, he stood. "If you'll excuse me, I need to go pack."

CHAPTER 4

Virginia rolled over, laying her ear up to the light-blue wall. In the next room, she heard Reuben moving around. His muffled sounds comforted her, and she hugged herself, recalling their time on the porch.

She wasn't sure Saloma's plan to show him how well they got along would work, but she couldn't help but take notice of him studying her earlier. For a split second, she recognized the look in his eyes. A wanting, almost yearning to be close to her.

Was she exaggerating his response? Maybe she was reading more into his abrupt departure? She could only surmise that her being there brought back memories of what they once shared. If only she knew who the girl was that had captured his attention. Maybe then she'd know what she was up against.

Pulling a pillow tight, she hugged it, pretending it was Reuben she held. A lump settled in the back of her throat, and she thought. *Where did I go wrong? I was sure we were moving along nicely. We had so much in common. Well, except for books and all.*

Without warning, she sat up and muttered, her breath coming quick and shallow with nervousness, "That's it! *Gott's* giving me another chance. Only He could orchestrate something like this. I thought it was all Saloma and my mother. But no...it must be some divine intervention."

She settled back down, pulling the heavy quilt to her chin, and prayed. *"Lord, I won't mess it up, I promise. You've given me another chance to prove to him I'm the one. Please, turn his heart back to me. Amen."*

***

Reuben wadded up yet another piece of paper and tossed it in the trash. He didn't understand why he was having such a hard time writing Allie a note explaining the plan change. Laying the tablet aside, he moved to the window. Oh, how he wished he had time to talk to her in person.

Under the darkened sky dotted with bright lights, he couldn't help but imagine what it would be like when the two of them were married. He wouldn't need to crawl into a cold bed by himself and wouldn't fall prey to one of his mother's schemes.

Just the thought of what his mother pulled left him feeling bitter. It gave him anxiety just thinking about the tension that would arise if his mother continued to butt her head into things that were no concern of hers. How could he protect Allie when he couldn't even protect himself?

There had been a time when his mother's opinion meant the world to him, and he liked pleasing her. Being the youngest and with so many years between him and his older siblings, they had a closeness that the other *kinner* didn't have. He tried to remember when things changed.

It had to be around the time he broke it off with Virginia. Looking back, he probably shared too much with his mother. Undoubtedly, she liked Virginia and was visibly upset when he broke the news.

He breathed in the crisp, clean air through the open window and scolded himself for being too forthcoming when it came to his mother. He was shy and reserved to a fault, except regarding his relationship with his mother. And now, when he wanted different things that didn't include her, she became upset and unyielding to his choices. How could he blame her? She was losing her last child, and like a lioness fighting for her cub, she had all claws open and ready to attack.

The problem was he wouldn't let her harm Allie or stand in their way of pursuing a life together. He snickered and thought. *Mamm won't know what hit her when she meets Allie. She's different from Virginia and certainly won't allow her to have the upper hand.* With an unsettled concern rumbling inside, he went back to his letter.

***

Morning came early, and with no time to stop by Allie's, Reuben slipped his letter in the mailbox before climbing into Elwin's truck.

Crates of apples had been loaded and secured in the truck bed, leaving just enough room for three suitcases tucked behind the seat. As Reuben slid beside Virginia, he groaned at the thought of sitting so close for almost twenty hours. He barely had room to stretch his long legs out, let alone having no space to get comfortable.

Virginia cleared her throat and smoothed her dark blue dress over her knees. "It's a little tight, but I promise I won't take up much room."

His expression was completely impersonal, but he couldn't help but think, *We didn't even sit this close in my courting buggy.*

Elwin pushed his elbows out. "I've got plenty of room." He tapped his shoulder on Virginia's. "Besides, I'd say sitting next to a pretty girl for twenty hours is a dream come true."

Reuben didn't need to see Virginia's look because the truck's air turned cold as ice with Elwin's outlandish remark. But he expected as much. His cousin was prone to speak whatever was on his mind, regardless of whether it was inappropriate or not. He had spent too much time with their *Englisch* neighbors, leaving him outspoken in the most unflattering ways. Reuben made a mental note to talk with him about it on their first rest stop.

Virginia struggled with her seat belt, and instead of giving Reuben time to help, Elwin reached over her lap and clicked it in place. "There you go. As snug as a bug in a rug."

Reuben felt her pull away from Elwin's closeness and leaned onto his shoulder. He suspected she felt more comfortable with him since she barely knew Elwin. He exhaled and moved closer to the window. She whispered, "I'm sorry," and sat back upright.

"No problem. It's a tight fit, but we'll make it work."
He sensed she was uncomfortable with the arrangement and tried to reassure her by lessening his grip on the door handle and stretching his legs out. When his thigh met hers, he didn't jerk it away like before but moved it aside slowly.

Her body language softened.

Elwin pulled out onto the road and flipped the radio on. "Music?"

Neither of them answered as Elwin scanned the channels. When he stopped on a slow country song, he bellowed out the song as if he'd written it himself. Surprisingly, he knew every word, and his voice kept in tune with the artist. The sun had yet to make it up over the horizon, so only the lights from the dashboard lit the cab. Even so, it was just enough light to see Virginia's shock as Elwin's voice carried the tune.

Reuben was almost embarrassed for Virginia as Elwin leaned in close and sang the words as if he was singing them just for her.

"You had me from "Hello," I felt love start to grow. The moment I looked in your eyes, you won me. It was over from the start...you completely stole my heart..."

Reuben reached up and turned the channel. "Perhaps we should find something else."

"Suit yourself. It's a long trip, and we might as well find something to keep us entertained." He tapped his thumbs on the steering wheel and asked Virginia, "What do you like to listen to?"

"Me?" shrugging her shoulders, she replied, don't get much opportunity to hear the radio. Occasionally, our driver plays a Christian station. I guess I've enjoyed that a time or two."

Elwin instructed Reuben. "Try 107.9. We should be able to pick up the Christian station out of Pittsburgh until we get to West Virginia." He paused until he found the station and continued. "I listen to anything except rap and heavy metal. That's a little too much even for this Amish kid."

It only took a few seconds before Elwin started to follow along with the words, singing in complete harmony to the voice on the radio.

Even Reuben was impressed and commented, "I didn't know you could sing."

Elwin snickered. "Neither did I. But it seems I'm natural at it. I've even gotten pretty good at the guitar." He looked over his shoulder. "I brought it along. It's under that blanket. Maybe I'll play it for you when we get to Florida."

***

Obnoxious, she thought. He really is the most obnoxious boy she'd ever met. That was until Elwin opened his mouth and sang to her. Suddenly, he became interesting, and she wanted to hear more. He was different for sure and certain. Not well mannered like Reuben, but different in an almost tantalizing kind of way. Perhaps this trip won't be so bad after all.

However, it didn't take long for him to stop singing and say something that made the hair on the back of her neck stand up.

"So, tell me, Virginia. What are the girls like in Pinecraft? I hear some of them even wear *Englisch* bikinis. Is that true?"

Unexpectedly, she let out a small "tsk" before adding, "I wouldn't know such things. If they do, that is between them and *Gott*. I think it's a sin to show so much skin in public, and I would never subject myself to such gawking."

She folded her hands on her lap and continued. "I've been to the beach, and you should see how some young men stare at those women. It's almost a disgrace what some *Englisch* girls wear. Barely strings to cover themselves up."

Elwin let out a loud yelp. "That's what I'm talking about."

His frenzy of excitement caught her off guard, and she thought. *Oh my. What have I gotten myself into?*

Turning slightly toward Reuben, she noticed he rolled his eyes in disbelief at his outburst. *Like night and day, the two of them*, she thought.

Confused about what they might have in common other than a family bloodline, she understood why Saloma refused to let her nephew come around. She's unsure how or why she agreed to let Reuben ride to Florida with him. But then she smiled internally. They both wanted the same thing. For her to become part of the Raber family. And much like Saloma, Virginia made it a mission to start taking back what was rightfully hers, regardless of the cost.

***

Elwin flashed an ironic smile Reuben's way when he threw him a stern expression. He couldn't care less that his stoic cousin had difficulty expressing himself. He quite liked standing out in the crowd. And he certainly didn't mind watching Virginia squirm at his boldness.

That was the problem with most Amish girls. They had no sense of adventure and let their prim and proper upbringing stifle any fun they might have.

And he didn't care what Reuben thought. He was a teenage boy prone to less than wholesome thoughts like the next. One being that he wouldn't mind seeing little Miss Virginia in one of those *Englisch* bathing suits. Just the idea left him imagining things he shouldn't be conjuring up. He shook his head, trying to chase away his raging attention as he chastised himself for allowing such things to enter his mind.

He turned the radio up to drown out the image and joined along with the song playing. He noticed Virginia tapping her fingers to the beat and smiled when she glanced his way.

He stopped singing long enough to ask, "Catchy beat, *jah*?"

"*Jah*, I like it."

Her smile warmed, and for a fleeting moment, he thought music might be a way to get her to lighten up a bit. When he held her gaze longer than she was comfortable with, or more than he should keep his eyes off the road, she flushed and looked away.

***

Saloma washed the last breakfast dishes and dried her hands on a towel, checking the time as she slipped her shoes on. The mailman delivered the mail precisely at ten, and she had a stack of letters to go out. Flipping through the pile as she walked to the mailbox, she wondered who had lifted the flag.

Retrieving the already stamped letter before placing her own in the box, she exclaimed, "Seriously? Well, I think not." Squinting against the morning sun, she looked toward the barn before folding the letter in half and tucking it in her sweater sleeve.

Saloma's irritation grew as she walked back to the *haus*. For a flirting second, she contemplated reading what Reuben had written, but instead, she grabbed one of Daniel's lighters from the drawer. Standing over the sink, she set it afire and washed its remains down the drain.

Something nagged at her conscience, but she pushed it away and resumed peeling apples. The thought of Reuben breaking it off with Virginia raised a fresh flurry of emotions inside of her, something she hadn't expected to feel so strongly about. Maybe this thing with Allie Mast was just a passing crush. She could only hope as much.

Daniel came inside to refill his coffee mug and asked, "What's burning?" Before focusing on the oil lamp above the table, he walked past the stove and checked the burners. "Smells like paper burning."

"Umm…" she stuttered, "Umm, I had problems lighting the stove and used a piece of paper."

She held her breath until her lie satisfied his curiosity. Without another word, he pulled out a chair and flipped the battery-operated weather radio on the hutch behind his chair.

After listening intently to the projected weather forecast for their immediate area, he changed the channel until he found an update for the hurricane moving toward Florida.

"Elwin should be able to get there and back before the worst of the storm hits. I should have held off for a few days. I'm having second thoughts about sending them before the storm. I hope the boy is smart enough to get out of there before it gets bad."

Concern bubbled up, and Saloma asked, "Will Reuben and Virginia be safe? Maybe we should call them back."

She laid her knife aside and retrieved her address book from the drawer beside the refrigerator. "I have Elwin's cell phone number written down somewhere. I could go to the phone shanty and call them."

"Now, just sit back down," Daniel demanded as he placed the radio back on the hutch. "Elwin might be reckless and sitting on the fence about some things, but the boy is a good driver. And besides, Reuben is smart about such things. They make a good team, and I have no doubt they'll keep a watchful eye on the sky. I guess I was just second-guessing my decision momentarily."

Daniel grabbed a handful of cut apple slices and kissed Saloma on the cheek before going back outside.

It wasn't until he left that she relaxed. She'd done and said many things she wasn't proud of. But outright lying to her husband left her writhing in shame.

CHAPTER 5

A llie fixed her eyes on the last day's sunlight fading across the floor as she set aside the small embroidery project she'd been working on. Sylvia had turned in early, leaving her to enjoy the day's quiet alone. Glancing out the window, the sky turned a pretty shade of rose as the day dipped below the horizon.

Moving to the open screen door, she welcomed in the cool evening air long enough to allow tiny goosebumps to move up her arms. Rubbing them away, she closed the door and flipped the lock. Not that there was a need to secure the door, she did so anyway because Sylvia felt better knowing they were locked in for the night.

Settling down on the small loveseat, she pulled her knees up under herself and picked up a book. The small-town Christian romance she was reading took her places she'd never been. This one took her to the grape vineyards of France.

Oh...how she wished she could visit there someday. Sitting in a small café on the cobblestone streets of Pérouges to the beaches of Saint-Jean-Cap-Ferrat sounded heavenly.

She couldn't help but giggle when she remembered Reuben rolling his eyes when she mentioned her travel plans to him. In his typical sensible way, he reminded her that his Old Order community didn't allow for air travel, and it would be impossible to hire a driver for a trip of that magnitude.

At the time, she hadn't thought much about it, but now, a pang of irritation settled in as she thought back to the exchange. It was awfully presumptuous of him to assume they would stay Old Order and not opt for her more liberal Mennonite background. It was the one topic they had yet to approach in any detail.

Losing all interest in reading, she closed the book and rubbed her temples. It had been a long day, and after her aunt informed her Virginia was taking an extended vacation and her workdays would be getting longer, she needed to go to sleep as well.

***

A tremendous sense of gratitude in her aunt's greeting that morning warmed Allie's heart. Balancing one of her grandchildren on her hip, she gave Allie her to-do list for the day.

"I can't thank you enough for taking on so much of Virginia's duties for the next few weeks. I don't know what I'd do without you." The middle-aged woman moved to the schedule calendar on the wall behind the cash register. "Now, Barbara Wagler is going to pick up a few of Virginia's shifts, but other than that, it will be just you and your uncle most days." She wiped the toddler's nose with a tissue and asked, "Are you sure you're up for it? I know it's asking a lot."

"I'm sure. But may I ask a favor from you?"

"Certainly. What is it?"

"Do you think it would be a problem to continue to send my agreed upon pay to my mother, but anything above that I could keep?"

She paused for a moment. "I don't see any problem with that." She nodded toward the fabric she'd seen Allie admiring earlier. "Are you saving for anything specific? Perhaps a few yards of that pretty white fabric?"

Allie felt her face flush slightly, unaware that her aunt had observed her marveling over the expensive fabric. When she ran her hand over the costly chiffon, she envisioned a lavish wedding dress.

Nothing too fancy, but long and flowing like some she had noticed in a bridal magazine she glanced through at the bookstore. Embarrassed that her aunt caught her swooning over the fabric, she quickly changed the subject. "I am saving for something special, but I don't think it will be like that fabric. It's way too expensive for me. Why are we carrying this type of fabric anyway?"

"Mrs. Hershberger ordered it, and that's what was left over. She was hired to make a wedding dress for an *Englisch* woman."

Allie returned to the table and picked up the bolt of fabric. "How much do you think is left on here?"

"Not sure, but since I highly doubt we'll ever sell the rest of it, you can take the rest at cost if you want."

Allie pulled the fabric up to her cheek. "It's so soft and silky."

"I'm serious. Take it if you want. You're about the only girl around who would be permitted to indulge in something so worldly. None of the young Amish girls would be permitted."

Allie quickly pulled the fabric off the cardboard bolt and folded it into a neat pile before her aunt changed her mind. "Please deduct the cost from my next pay."

The dress hovered in her mind for the rest of the day. Now that Reuben had asked her to be his wife, she was free to plan, and wedding attire was high on her priority list.

It was all she could do to get through the day and get home to start laying out a dress pattern. She'd have just enough time to take some measurements before she was due to meet Reuben at the bookstore. He mentioned that he needed to work late, and it wouldn't be until seven when he'd be free. She volunteered to walk into town to save time so he wouldn't have to come all the way out to get her.

***

The *Book Cellar* was unusually busy for a Friday night, and she had to wait a few minutes before securing a table near the window. She came early to have time to browse a few bridal magazines before Reuben arrived. She didn't want him to see what she had planned before their wedding.

Leafing through the pages, she stopped on a simple yet elegant A-lined dress that would fit her shape beautifully. While her conservative upbringing didn't allow for anything too fancy or ornate, it did allow for something extra special. And she certainly didn't want to shock Reuben too much since his *g'may* only allowed simple solid colors and dresses that could double as a church dress.

She retrieved her notebook from her bag, jotted down some ideas, and drew a replica of the simple yet classy calf-length dress. It was perfect, and she got all jittery inside just thinking about how pretty it would be.

She took a sip of her coffee and looked around the room. Each table was filled with other couples or friends whispering between them. All at once, she missed her friends in Sugarcreek. Shortly after moving to Willow Springs, she met Reuben, and nothing or no one else mattered since.

She had just started to get close to Virginia, and she would have loved to show her the dress in the magazine. Turning it over, she wondered if she should buy it to show her new friend. Gasping at the price, she decided it wasn't in her budget and placed the magazine back on the rack. Besides, she'd most likely have her dress made before Virginia made it back from vacation.

Resting her elbows on the small table, she held her mug in both hands and wondered what it would be like to have all of Reuben's sisters-in-law as family. He certainly had a slew of them, and she looked forward to getting to know each one. She'd always wanted to have a big family, and Reuben's held so many possibilities that she was giddy with excitement.

She wondered why Reuben hadn't offered to introduce her to his family. She knew little of his brothers or his parents. Perhaps that's why he insisted she not speak to anyone about his proposal. She washed the nagging question from her mind and conceded he must want to tell them together before the news got out.

Glancing down at her watch, she was alarmed when he was half an hour late. It wasn't like Reuben to be tardy, and without thinking twice, she picked up her bag and went outside. Sitting on the bench near the front door, she stared down Main Street, willing his buggy to appear over the small hill that led into town. When the last streetlight clicked on, she secured her bag over her shoulder and headed home, disappointed and concerned at his unusual behavior.

Once she got home, she sat on their small front porch and looked across the road toward the lane that led back to Raber's Farm & Produce. Nothing. No one came or left, as far as she could tell. Oh, how she wished she was brave enough to walk up and ask to see him. But she knew him well enough that there had to be a good explanation for why he didn't keep his date. Perhaps if he didn't get word to her by tomorrow evening, she would be daring enough to walk to the Raber farm and inquire for herself.

***

The next evening, despite her apprehension, Allie walked down the long lane that led back to Reuben's *haus*. All day, she had an overwhelming emptiness in the pit of her stomach that wouldn't go away. There wasn't any way she would let another twenty-four hours pass without knowing what happened.

In awe of the grandness of the two-story farmhouse and barns that surrounded the farm, she felt pretty small and unimportant. Reuben didn't talk much about his parents' business, but by the looks of the orchards surrounding the house, it was a much larger operation than she'd imagined.

As she passed one of the outbuildings, it looked like it was being set up for church services. The huge double doors were opened, and row after row of benches were neatly lined up inside. She couldn't help herself from walking in to admire the timber beam rafters and old pine-planked floor. She held her hands up to her chin and turned slowly in a circle, imagining what a wonderful space it would be to host a wedding.

Moving back outside, she scolded herself internally for her fairytale tendencies and chased any such notions far from her mind. Her mother often reminded her that things like that didn't happen in real life and that she needed to be more realistic about love and marriage. She tucked a few loose hairs back under her lace head covering as she moved toward the porch that wrapped around three sides of the Raber *haus*.

She took a deep breath and lightly knocked on the open screen door without letting it out. Overcome with an unusual nervousness, she lost all words when Reuben's mother came to the door.

The woman stopped about two feet from the door and stared at her through the screen. Neither of them said a word, and it was Allie who, only after she filled her lungs, asked, "Is Reuben home? I'd like to speak to him if I may."

The woman, who clearly Reuben favored, all except her stout shape, sneered at her in the most unwelcoming manner.

"He's not home," the woman snapped.

Allie checked her tone before she responded.

The last thing she wanted was to get on the woman's wrong side before they had been formally introduced. "May I inquire when you think he may return?"

"Couldn't say."

All moisture left Allie's mouth, but she was determined to not let the woman see her tone bothered her. "I'm Allie Mast. Reuben and I are friends." She paused long enough to lick her lips before proceeding. "He was supposed to meet me in town last night but never showed up. I was concerned he might be ill or something. It's not like him to keep me waiting without cause."

The woman continued to stand her ground and didn't offer for her to come inside. Most unusual for an Amish woman. "Reuben is plenty old enough, and it's not my job to keep track of his whereabouts."

The woman's stern face distorted disapprovingly, and Allie could practically feel the older woman hovering on the edge of frustration.

The two shared a long look. Almost as if one was waiting for the other to back down. Without a succession of emotion on either of their faces, Allie remained, unmoving.

Reuben's mother finally broke the stance. "You're a bit young to call on my boy, don't ya think? Not sure how you do things where you come from, but showing up at a young man's *haus* uninvited is much too bold and forthright." Without letting Allie answer, the woman continued. "Do your parents know you're sharing the company of men much too old for you?"

"*Jah*, my mother knows who I'm spending time with, as do my aunt and uncle."

"I've seen you at Shetler's Grocery."

"*Jah*, I've come to help my aunt and uncle for a while in the store."

"Well, I have work to do, and I can't be here standing here all evening."

In all her days, Allie never dreamed Reuben's mother would be so rude and uninviting. It was like she had a vendetta against her, and she didn't know why.

For goodness' sake, they had only spoken a few words at the grocery store until a few minutes ago. There was no doubt that the woman was about to give her not so much as an inkling of Reuben's whereabouts. "When he does return, would you mind telling him I stopped by to check on him?"

Silence was met with her unanswered question, and Reuben's mother shut the door without saying another word.

* * *

Daniel closed the newspaper and asked, "Who was at the door?"

With a heavy breath, Saloma moaned, "Allie Mast of all people. I can't believe she had the nerve to call on Reuben uninvited."

Daniel was trying to be understanding, but by the way his *fraa* was acting, he knew she was anything but hospitable toward the girl. "I take it you didn't invite her in?"

"Invite her into my home? Why on earth would I do that?"

Daniel weighed his words before answering. "Would have been to show her a little compassion, I suppose." He set the paper aside and settled back in his chair. "I told you before to let it be. Quit trying to play *Gott* with their lives."

Saloma gathered the dishes from the table and dropped them in the sink, splashing water on the floor. She wiped the spill and spat, "And I told you, you keep worrying about keeping food on the table and let me take care of family matters."

In the worst way, Daniel wanted to honor his wife, but he knew that if he didn't get a handle on her actions, there would be more trouble to pay. He stood and held out a hand to help her up from the floor. "I'm standing my ground on this topic. I won't tolerate you being rude to the girl. And secondly, I won't have you poking your nose into Reuben's life choices. You're dishonoring *Gott*, and I won't have it."

Saloma shook her hand from his and took a seat. After wiping her brow with the back of her hand, she snarled, "Go! I have work to do, and you're in my way!"

Defeated by her response, Daniel pushed his chair under the table, scraping the hardwood floor along the way, and stomped toward the door. Looking back at the woman he'd been married to for a better part of his life, he tried to pinpoint when life had turned so ugly for her. Over the last few years, her disposition seemed to worsen, making him question himself. *Perhaps I didn't do her any justice by allowing it to happen. Instead of pointing out her scrupulous behavior, I turned the other way. In doing so, I failed to set healthy boundaries regarding family issues.* He shook his head, grabbed his jacket off the peg by the door, and as the door slammed shut whispered, "How on earth am I ever going to get a hold of this?" He remembered something his *datt* always said when he had to deal with a difficult situation. *There may be short-term pain, but the reward is a long-term gain.*

He hoped that was the case in this instance because if he didn't control Saloma, he half expected a visit from the bishop.

***

Cringing from the sound of Daniel's departure, Saloma took a long, calming breath. The dizziness in her head took longer than usual to fade, and she took the damp dish towel and held it over her eyes. A heaviness settled over her when she recalled the disgust on her husband's face. A small part of her yearned for the closeness they once had, and she couldn't help but blame herself for the coldness in his eyes.

Recognizing the part she played in the tension hovering in the air was too much to bear, so instead, she pushed herself up from the table and forged on with her plans to stop Allie Mast from wedging her way into the Raber family.

First and foremost, she needed to write to her cousin in Sugarcreek to find out what kind of family she came from. If the rumor she heard about her mother was true, the young girl was latching onto Reuben, hoping to wiggle her way into an affluent family. She'd undoubtedly bring it to Reuben's attention if that was the case. Furthermore, she'd be barking up the wrong tree if she knew Raber's financial affairs accurately.

***

Daniel studied the stack of invoices strewed across his desk. In recent years, it had gotten harder and harder to make ends meet. While Saloma was distraught over Reuben's choice to leave the farm, he, on the other hand, was grateful he didn't need to find a way to support another boy's family. If he didn't find another way to generate farm income, he'd be forced to ask some of his sons to look for work elsewhere. If he didn't come up with a plan soon, the tradition of Raber Farms would soon be lost for good.

He sat back and lit his pipe and thought. *If only I could find a way to generate new income.* He blew a circle of smoke out and mumbled, "At this rate, I'll never compete with larger operations."

He balanced his pipe between his teeth, stuffed the worrisome invoices in a folder, and pushed them away. "Out of sight, out of mind," he whispered.

As he walked to where a few of his sons had gathered near the barn, he heaved a sigh and thought. *It's about time I stopped bearing this burden alone. They all need to know what's going on. Perhaps we could all put our heads together and come up with a solution.*

CHAPTER 6

Clouds weaved cobwebs across the moon as Elwin pulled the truck into Virginia's grandmother's driveway in Pinecraft, Florida. Asleep on his shoulder, Reuben elbowed Virginia. "We're here."

Reuben rubbed his shoulder and stepped out of the truck. The air was thick and moist as he breathed in an overwhelming sweet aroma he couldn't place.

Virginia stopped for Elwin to retrieve her suitcase from behind the seat and stated, "Oh, how I've missed that smell." She moved to the row of reddish-orange flowers climbing up and over the white fence at the front of her grandmother's yard. She bent to take in its pleasantness. "It's cape honeysuckle, and I just love it."

Reuben looked over at his cousin, rolled his eyes, and let a furrow settle across his forehead. He'd spent the better part of a full day cramped up in a truck, let alone the last eight hours bearing the weight of Virginia on his shoulder. The last thing he wanted was to smell a sickening sweet flower. Handing her the suitcase, he mumbled, "Enjoy your visit."

"You'll be here for a few weeks, *jah*?" She rested her hand on his forearm. "I'm hoping you'll allow me to show you around some."

Dismayed, he jerked his arm free. "Like I said before, I doubt I'll have much time for such things."

She leaned in closer. "All work and no play isn't good for the soul."

Reuben clenched his jaw. Her body language was alarming, and he wondered where she'd gotten her boldness all the sudden. In the shadow of the streetlight, she threw him a sly smile and retrieved a key from its hiding spot and disappeared inside.

Elwin started the truck and smirked. "I think you have your hands full with that one. I thought you said she was quiet and reserved. I don't see that at all." Elwin pulled out onto the street and nosed his way through the avenues. "She's got spunk, and I like it!"

Reuben rubbed his chin. "Not sure what's gotten into her. She's never acted like that before."

"If you ask me, she's on a mission."

"A mission? What might that be?"

Elwin leered. "Come on! Don't be so blind. It didn't take a fool to see precisely what she's up to." He paused for a moment. "That and the way she slithered up close to you all the way here."

"She did no such thing."

"You're the one who was all jammed up against the door. I had plenty of room on my side."

Reuben stiffened. "Well, she's in for a rude awakening. I've come here for one reason and one reason only."

Elwin laughed. "If I didn't need to get this load delivered and back to Pennsylvania by Thursday, I'd wager a little bet and watch how it plays out."

Reuben pointed toward the sky. "Maybe you'll get out of here. Look at those clouds."

Not even a sliver of the moon remained behind the dark clouds that ushered in twilight. Driving slowly through the quiet neighborhood, Elwin concentrated on finding the address on Gilbert Street to their uncle's house. The paved street curved past Pinecraft Park and abruptly ended, forcing them to turn around. After locating the one-story sand colored house on the opposite end of the street, Elwin pulled off to the side, shut the engine off and turned toward Reuben. "Should we wake him?"

Before the words barely got out of his mouth, lights from the porch invited them in.

The spitting image of his father, Reuben and Elwin's Uncle John, ushered them to the kitchen. "I was up early checking the weather and I heard you pull in." He glanced out the small window over the sink. "You'll need to get that load to the produce market right away."

Elwin stretched. "As soon as I grab a couple winks, I'll get right to it."

The short, rotund man filled a large mug with dark brew and replied, "Sorry, son. Storm's due to roll in by forenoon and they'll want to get the market boarded up." John took a seat at the table. "Best you down that coffee and get busy."

John turned toward Reuben. "You can help me get the *haus* boarded up this morning. They've already evacuated vacationers and all that's left is us locals."

John held up a finger and listened to the report broadcast over the radio. *Residents are advised to prepare for the storm surge to come on land approximately at eleven thirty this morning. All residents of Sarasota County are urged to take shelter in one of the many storm shelters across the county at once. Otherwise, stay inside, away from windows and doors. If your home is in one of the low laying areas, you are advised to take shelter at the nearest Red Cross location immediately.*

Both boys looked warily at their uncle, and Reuben asked, "Are you in one of those low laying areas?"

"*Jah.* As soon as we get the *haus* closed, we'll head over to the elementary school. It's on higher ground there."

Elwin took the last swig of coffee and stood. "I'll head over to the market and get these apples unloaded and be back to help shortly."

The overwhelming need for sleep turned into adrenaline as Reuben followed his uncle outside. "What's first?" he asked.

"Go grab the window shutters from the garage, and I'll double check the generator. We'll need to put all the lawn furniture away and set those big potted plants on their side."

John stopped to stack chairs. "I filled sandbags yesterday and we'll put them at all the doors before we leave."

They had boarded up all the windows and secured everything in the garage in no time. Elwin pulled back up to the house just as they were placing the last of the sandbags against the front door.

Reuben handed the drill to John and looked toward the sky. "Everything seems so quiet. Do you think the storm might have turned and gone back out to sea?"

John took off his hat and wiped his forehead with the back of his arm. "This is just the calm before the storm. The wind will start to pick up anytime now. We best get to the shelter."

They didn't even let Elwin get out of the truck before they climbed inside. John held his small dog on his lap and secured his lead while giving Elwin directions.

The side streets were crowded with cars and golf carts all headed to the same location. "I guess I wasn't the only one who waited until the last minute." The older man paused before adding. "Seems like ever since Martha died last year, I tend to have a hard time organizing such things. She was the one who kept us in line."

Reuben caught a flash of sadness in his uncle's face, and for some reason, he felt apologetic even when there was no need to. It was *Gott's* will that his Aunt Martha was called home so quickly, and they all needed to accept it. Furthermore, what right did they have to question *Gott's* timing?

Reuben didn't comment but reached over and patted the nervous dog on the head. "Why is she acting so strange?"

John lovingly rubbed the dog's underside. "She must feel the drop in barometric pressure. She typically gets anxious right before a storm." He pulled the dog closer. "Martha was the only one who could calm her down. Her death was hard on both of us."

All Reuben could say was, "Sorry."

"Death is hard, but loneliness is tougher," his uncle remarked.

It had only been two days since Reuben had seen Allie, and he already missed her. He couldn't imagine what it would be like to miss someone you'd been married to for over thirty years. "Do you try to keep busy?" he asked.

"It's about all I can do. That's half the reason why I needed your help. I took on too much work trying to keep my mind occupied," his uncle said.

"I'm happy to help." Reuben raised his eyebrow and rolled down the window. "What's that noise?"

"Those are the hurricane sirens." John bent down slightly to peer out the window. "Wind's starting to pick up."

Elwin nodded his head in the direction of stopped traffic ahead. "Is that the school?"

"*Jah*, just follow those cars."

***

By the time they had parked and headed inside, the wind picked up so strongly it blew Reuben's straw hat to the ground. Running to retrieve it, he ran right into Virginia and her grandmother.

"Reuben, thank goodness you made it. *Grossmommi* says we'll be safe here."

Without hesitating, he took the elderly woman's elbow, trying to shield her from the wind, as they made their way inside. Virginia followed close behind, carrying a small bag and a carrier with a wailing cat.

Helping the woman to one of the cots that had been set up along the wall, Reuben turned toward Virginia at her comment. "Things are working out perfectly for us to spend some time together. Looks like we will have a lot of time to catch up while we wait out the storm."

Remembering what Elwin had said about her motives, the first stir of suspicion edged its way up the back of his neck. Making sure the older woman was comfortable before he responded gave him a few seconds to gather his thoughts.

Exasperated beyond words, he took Virginia by the hand and led her to the opposite side of the room. When he stopped to face her, the look in her eyes was soft and alluring. "Stop," he whispered.

Her light tone didn't seem to fit the moment, which aggravated him even more. "I haven't a clue what you're talking about."

He uttered a surly grunt. "You know exactly what you're doing, and we're going to put a stop to it right here and now."

Once again, she inappropriately laid her fingers on his arm, forcing him to snarl a response. "That is what I'm talking about! I'm not sure what you have conjured up, but I've just about had enough."

"But Reuben, we were so good together," she pleaded. "Couldn't we at least try to make it work again? I thought maybe getting away from Willow Springs would give us the chance to see if there was anything left worth building on."

He lowered his voice as a family settled in beside them. "The only thing I'll be building is furniture." His harsh tone didn't sit well with his conscience, and he tempered his voice. "I know your plans didn't line up with mine, and I'm sorry about that. But I've moved on. I wish you would do the same."

Her blue eyes brimmed with tears, mingled with sorrow and remorse. "Don't we owe it to ourselves to try? What happens if we regret our choices a year down the road?"

Reuben shifted to the other foot and crossed his arms over his chest. "I suppose that's the chance I'll have to take."

Without warning, her face flushed furiously, and she turned on her heel and left in a huff.

Finally, he exhaled and looked around the room to locate Elwin and his uncle.

***

Virginia sat on the floor, leaned on the wall, and pulled her knees up to her chest. Her grandmother had stretched out on the cot and closed her eyes, leaving her unaccompanied with her thoughts. Pulling the cat crate closer, she whispered calming words to Maxi, trying to quiet her discomfort. Her thoughts were spinning out of control. *If only I knew who I was up against. Perhaps then I'd know what to do. I've asked all my friends, and no one seems to know who he's seeing. It must be someone outside of the g'may.*

The stuffy gymnasium echoed with an array of muffled voices as she gazed around the room looking for Reuben and Elwin. Like herself, a few evacuees carried small pets in carriers as did Reuben's Uncle John. The small dog barked relentlessly, and she noticed Reuben trying to silence it.

Even from across the room, Reuben's lanky stature enticed her. She turned her face away and landed her eyes on Elwin. Much like his cousin, Elwin was slender and lean, but had a mystery about him. A thought swiftly came to mind. *That's it! A way to a man's heart is to make him think he's missing out on a good thing. Perhaps I could entice Elwin's help with this.*

With a new plan looming, she went back to making sure her grandmother was comfortable.

***

The lights flickered, and a wave of wind hit the side of the building, leaving everyone in the dark for a few minutes. A hush fell over the gymnasium, which ended when the generator kicked into action, promoting a ripple of relief throughout the room.

Elwin was suddenly filled with a sense of uneasiness. He sat on the cot's edge and leaned his elbows on his knees, clasping his hands together. "Sounds awful out there. Are you sure this old building will hold up?"

John's expression lingered. "I've been through a few of these. But this one is expected to be a Category 4. Winds could reach 130 miles per hour."

Elwin listened with obvious concern as John continued. "It's the storm surge that worries me the most. We live in a low tide area, so not too sure what we'll find when it passes."

Reuben frowned in genuine alarm and asked, "How long do you think it will keep up?"

Before John had time to answer, a Red Cross worker came by and handed them all a permanent black marker and exclaimed. "Write your name and next of kin's phone number on your arm."

Both boys looked alarmed and did as they were told. An eerie sound circled the building as a hush fell over the room. For the next three hours, families sat in huddled groups, some praying, some crying, all cringing as flying debris hit the side of the school building.

Four hours later, the Red Cross worker's announcement that the right-front quadrant of the storm had finally passed broke the defeating trance. To the long-time residents of Florida, this meant that the storm was over, and they could evaluate the damage.

John was the first to move to the door, exclaiming, "We might as well see what we're up against." As he tried to push the door open, a resistance prevented him from doing so.

Elwin and Reuben helped release the door, and a small wave of water splashed around their feet. Once again, an announcement warned the residents of surging water and rising tides and encouraged everyone to stay put until emergency personnel could evaluate the surrounding area.

Stepping over a small wall of sandbags, all three men and a group who followed them surveyed the damage in front of them. John noticed Elwin's overturned truck and several golf carts stacked in the open parking lot. "I guess we know what all that noise was now."

Elwin let out a few explicit *Englisch* words to the alarm of both Reuben and John. When Reuben showed his disgust by rolling his eyes, Elwin shouted, "Don't give me that look. You didn't just pay two thousand dollars for a new paint job. That box truck is my bread and butter. No truck. No job." He continued to let words flow from his mouth in the most unbecoming manner, and Reuben looked over his shoulder, hoping none of the women had followed them outside.

John followed them both to the parking lot. "It won't be anything to upturn it. After the streets are cleared, tow trucks will scour the streets for things like this. But that won't happen anytime soon. We have more important things to deal with."

Reuben turned his ear to listen carefully and held his hand up to quiet them both. "Do you hear that? Sounds like someone is crying."

Both boys took off running toward the sound. As they approached the other side of the overturned truck, an old minivan nested up against the truck lay on its side. "Oh my!" Reuben yelled. "There's people in there." As all three men worked to free the family, a group gathered.

***

Throughout the whole ordeal, Virginia didn't take her eyes off Reuben and his family. Especially Elwin. He held the clue to figure out how she could get Reuben to change his mind. If anyone could tell her what it would take, it would be the one person he spent the most time with. She stood at the back of the crowd and watched Elwin climb on the overturned van, struggle to open the door, and hand down a small child to his waiting uncle. When the child continued crying, she ran to his side and pulled him into her arms. It didn't take but a few moments of whispering calming words in the small girl's ear for her to relax. After two more children and their parents were freed, Virginia handed the small child back to her mother.

Elwin moved to her side. "It's amazing no one was hurt."

Virginia agreed and nodded toward the collection of toppled vehicles. "Your truck prevented the van from being swept into the street. The school sits higher, and if it had been blown into the street, *Gott* only knows where it might have landed."

His voice took on a low and serious tone. "I guess you're right. I hate to think what could have happened. "

Virginia smiled and replied, "I say the good Lord knew faithfully what would happen." She lingered a few seconds before adding, "Could be He sent you all the way to Florida just so your big truck could save that one family."

CHAPTER 7

S aloma tucked her cousin's letter in her pocket and continued to make supper. If Daniel found out she'd written inquiring about Allie, he would be furious, to say the least. But wasn't it a mother's right to protect her children? Daniel wouldn't see it that way; she was certain of that.

After placing a platter of meatloaf in the center of the table, Saloma took her place next to Daniel and asked, "So tell me why you've called the boys over tonight. Is there something going on I should know about?"

He replied slightly condescendingly, "You'll find out along with the *kinner* once they arrive."

Saloma stiffened momentarily at his response and cautiously stated, "I'd prefer not to be kept in the dark."

He lifted one eyebrow and replied, "That goes both ways."

Alarmed at his strange statement, Saloma asked, "What's that supposed to mean?"

Daniel buttered a slice of bread and scowled. "Bishop Weaver paid me a visit forenoon."

Saloma dropped her fork and scurried to retrieve it from the floor. "*Ach*. What did he want?"

Daniel firmly grabbed her hand. "We spoke about a few things, but what has me concerned is you prying into matters that don't concern you."

She shook her hand away. "I'm only trying to help."

His voice escalated. "No, you're forcing the bishop to remind me that I don't have my house in order and that I best get you under control before I'm taken before the other ministers."

Heat rose up Saloma's neck; it took all she had to control her emotions. She knew full well it was her husband's job to deal with such things. But Mose went too far. How dare he go to Daniel about their conversation? Didn't he know she could ruin his good name in a matter of minutes? The Weaver family was highly regarded throughout Willow Springs and the Amish community. However, she was one of the few who knew the truth.

Silence descended as she weighed her words carefully. "It's the bishop's place to keep his flock in order. And that includes Reuben."

Saloma noticed Daniel's chest expanding. He wasn't one to let such things upset him, but she could tell by his sudden tautness she was overstepping grace.

With a sharp exhalation of his breath, he spat. "I'll not hear of you going behind my back to speak to the bishop again. Is that clear?"

She mumbled in a somewhat strangled voice, "I'll keep my concerns to myself and not bother him again."

The words escaped her lips, but she knew she couldn't keep the promise not to handle the situation as she saw fit. It was all she could do not to rip her cousin's letter from her pocket, hoping to discover anything she could use in her defense.

Two older boys bounded through the back door and comfortably sat at the table. Saloma pulled the breadbasket away, eyeing how dirty and sweaty they were from working the back fields all day. "Don't you have any manners? Go wash up first!"

Saloma didn't need to look over her shoulder at Daniel. She felt his eyes burn condemning holes in her back with her sharp tone. While the boys might not notice the strain between them, there was no mistake; she'd pushed her husband a bit too far this time.

***

Daniel pushed his plate away and leaned back in his chair. After holding his coffee cup up for Saloma to fill, he asked the boys about their progress on the north field.

"How long before you have that old orchard cleared and ready to plow under?"

His eldest son, Almer, positioned a piece of meatloaf between two slices of bread and answered, "We removed the last stump today. We can start working the ground after we get the brush burned." After taking a bite, he continued. "Still have plenty of time before snow hits."

Daniel rolled his comment through his head, calculating the cost of buying trees in time for spring planting. That would give him about five months before he would need to come up with funds.

Once the rest of the boys showed up, he sucked in a long drag from his pipe and exhaled, hoping the tobacco would clear his head before he delivered his news.

Almer wiped his mouth with the back of his hand. "So, can we get on with this? I have chores waiting at home." Much like his *mamm*, Almer felt as if the world revolved around him and held little patience for idle chit-chat.

Daniel clucked his tongue. "There's no easy way to say this. We've struggled to keep up with Curtman's Apple Orchard and Cider Mill in Erie. Seems they undercut our prices on just about everything."

Almer's tone grew cutting. "Their operation is three times as big as ours. We'll never be able to compete with them. Besides, I hear they're making hard cider now. We can't compete with that."

Daniel's voice became serious. "No, we can't, and I have no desire to. But we do need to put our heads together and develop a way to generate a new income stream." He paused long enough for the boys to comprehend the severity of their situation. "If we don't, I'm afraid some of you boys will be forced to look for work elsewhere."

Saloma quickly inserted her two cents, directing her comment toward Daniel as she stood to carry a bowl to the sink. "I knew it! If you had forced Reuben to help on the farm, we might not be in this situation."

Daniel didn't need to respond. Almer was swift to set the record straight. "That would have only put another man on the payroll. Reuben might be the smartest one of us all."

Taking the pipe from his mouth, Daniel used it to direct her to sit down. "Unless you have something constructive to add."

With a look of defeat on her face, Daniel noticed he had spoken too harshly to his *fraa*. He didn't like what the day's challenges had done to his disposition, and he'd be sure to rectify it later. He'd need to come up with a better way to address their differences, regardless of how much her actions had frustrated him of late.

With reluctance in his voice, he continued. "We have five months before we need to foot the bill for two hundred new apple trees. Elwin took a load of apples to Florida, and we have six more deliveries waiting as soon as he returns. We have five tons promised to the canning facility in Pittsburgh and plenty left over to stock the produce stand for the next eight weeks."

Almer asked, "Did you consider the cider mill sales?"

"I did. But we will need to raise our prices per gallon by two dollars to cover the rising cost of fuel to generate the press and plastic jugs."

Saloma piped in. "Two dollars? Customers will complain, for sure."

"Do you have another idea about how we can absorb the cost?"

"Well, no. Not at this moment, but there must be another way."

Almer tapped his thumb on the table. "What if we went to some area grocery stores and asked them to carry our cider?"

Daniel balanced his pipe between his teeth and nodded. "That will help, but cider doesn't bring in enough sales. We need more wholesale apple crate orders."

"It's time we thought about expanding our produce line." Almer suggested in a thoughtful tone.

"I've thought of that," Daniel replied, "but we should have talked about that in the spring. Not now when planting season is over."

Almer leaned back, his eyes unblinking. "I wish you would have come to us earlier."

"I'm thinking cabbage," Daniel stated without acknowledging Almer's comment.

In a quick gesture of disgust, Saloma declared, "I'm not dealing with fields of stinky cabbage. For goodness' sake, Daniel, what are you thinking?"

Daniel ran a hand through his beard. "If we don't find another way to fatten our bank account, we'll be forced to sell off some acreage to pay the taxes by the first of the year."

Almer held up a cautioning hand to his parents. "Now, let's not put the cart before the horse. We've got five months before they're due. We'll find a solution by then."

Daniel cleared his throat and stood. "Go home to your families. It's getting late; I'm ready to call it a day. I'd prefer you not share this with your wives just yet. Let's see if we can come up with a solution first. No sense in worrying them."

***

After the boys left, Saloma tried to continue the conversation with Daniel, but he waved her off and headed to bed, leaving her ample time to read her cousin's letter.

Dear Saloma,

It's such a beautiful autumn day here in Sugarcreek, sunny and breezy. Just did laundry, and it shouldn't take long to dry. The maple leaves are starting to turn a beautiful red, and my mums are blooming beautifully. I've been busy canning the last of the garden and hope to finish up by making grape pie filling at week's end.

It was so lovely to hear from you. We should keep those letters coming more often. I must remember how much we have in common and how closely we share thoughts.

I was as dismayed as you over the plight of Reuben and his Mennonite friend. Heavens, what a tapestry! Weaving two people together like that clearly is not what the Lord has in mind. I see only strife for sure and certain.

Saloma smiled at Carla's choice of words and whispered to herself. "You get it. Why can't Daniel see what we see?"

You may need to tell Reuben about Simon and Marybelle. Do you remember them? That was Aunt Viola's middle boy. He ran off with a girl from another faith, and they never saw him again. Word has it they live on some remote island in Africa. Missionaries of sorts. Can barely make ends meet. And those kinner of theirs never even met their grandparents.

Saloma gasped at the memory and mumbled, "That's right. Simon married outside the Amish faith. Broke his poor *mamm's* heart. Certainly, it's what sent her to an early grave."

I just don't know what goes through these young people's heads these days. I can only imagine how worried you are about Reuben's plight. Can't they see what heartache falls upon a family when these choices are made without considering long-term consequences?

I found a Mennonite woman down the street who knew Allie's parents. Bert and Kathy Mast. Here to find out Kathy used to be Amish. My neighbor thinks her schwester still lives in Willow Springs. Do you know Leona Shetler?

You're not going to believe what I found out! Of all things, they are missionaries. As far as my neighbors can remember, their children spend time with relatives while they travel. They live in a small apartment over the diner when they're in town. She didn't know much about their children other than they had two daughters. I assume one of them is the girl you mentioned in your letter.

All I know is it raised an alarm when I remembered about Aunt Viola's boy. I'd hate to see that happen to you. You are doing exactly what you need to do, discouraging Reuben from moving forward with this girl. I don't know how it will work. Too many differences. Trouble, I tell you, trouble!

You may have thought of this, but do you think she's got wind of how affluent you and Daniel are in the community? If the poor girl longs for stability and financial security, perhaps she's hoping to find those things in the Raber family.

Saloma bobbed her head to agree and muttered, "My thoughts accurately."

All I know is if one of my boys were setting their eyes on someone outside the faith, I'd also be stepping in. My heart goes out to you, cousin. After one daughter and six boys who have stayed close by, I'd be fighting long and hard to keep the last one close as well. You have all my prayers. Let me know if there is anything else I can do for you.

Blessings,

Carla

Saloma folded the letter and slipped it into her bible. When her conscience crept in, she removed it and secured it in the book she was reading. She didn't dare take the chance of Daniel finding it.

Pushing the rocker chair with the ball of her foot, she let the gentle sway calm her racing mind. As the last remnant of daylight fell behind the horizon, she closed her eyes, hoping a plan would form in her mind. She was thankful she'd convinced John to lure Reuben to Florida. Daniel would be furious if he found out what part she played in all that. Plus, she finagled Virginia to visit her grandmother and Elwin to provide transportation. The only thing left was getting Allie to leave Willow Springs before Reuben returned.

But how she was going to do that was still a mystery. Suddenly, an idea floated across her mind, and she sat up straight and murmured. "Oh, no, I couldn't do that! Even for me, that's going too far."

She walked to the window and played the scenario over in her head while she watched the sky turn to night. Could she make it work and not get caught? It surely would take care of the problem. But if anyone found out what she'd done…oh my, she thought. *Daniel would be devastated.* Moving outside, she sat on the porch's top step and let the cool September air swirl around her bare feet.

All reasoning left her as she played out the consequences of carrying out her idea. The plan started coming together, and she plotted out the place and time to set it in motion. A wave of adrenaline filled her at the thought of finding a way to force Allie to move back to Sugarcreek. If Mose wouldn't help, Daniel felt she was meddling where she didn't belong, and Reuben didn't realize he was ruining his life; she was ready to do whatever it would take. Even if that meant she would jeopardize her name and status in the community. At least at the end of the day, she'd get what she wanted, and that was keeping Reuben from jumping the fence.

***

Daniel lay with his arm over his eyes. Too consumed with worry to sleep and too angry to speak with Saloma, he took in some long cleansing breaths.

He played the day over in his head. The visit from the bishop gave him one more challenge he didn't plan on that day. He was in utter shock at what the bishop shared. In all sense of the word, he was losing control, and Bishop Weaver wasn't shy in telling him so. If a man can't control his family, what good was it to be the head of the household? For the last year, Saloma had said and done things he never dreamed she'd do. He couldn't imagine what was going through her head. Headstrong was once a favorable attribute of hers, and he gladly let her take the lead on most things. But going above his head and taking their private problems to the bishop in the form of a threat—she'd gone too far this time.

He sighed. While he couldn't define the source of his unsettledness, the feeling continued to emerge until he remembered something Mose had said. "Man to man, I'm warning you. If Saloma thinks for one minute, she can use my family's past to benefit her wants and desires, she has another think coming. I won't allow her to dishonor my *schwester's* name. You can count on that. The past is the past, which is just where it will stay."

Before he left, Mose made it a point to hold out his leather notebook. "And as I told Saloma, my family isn't the only one who holds close to past mistakes."

The whole scene left Daniel disturbed. And even more now that he had time to sort out the meaning behind the bishop's warning. What did he collect in his little black book?

A slurry of thoughts entered Daniel's mind, but one stood out more than any other. *Does he know? No, he couldn't. I covered all my tracks, I'm sure of it. There's no way anyone could find out what I'd done.*

A persistent, cross-grained feeling engulfed him, and he stood and pushed the bed aside. On his knees, he moved the loose floorboard to reveal a small tin box. Stopping long enough to ensure he didn't hear Saloma's footsteps, he opened the box and breathed a sigh of relief when the hidden documents were secured right where he'd left them.

Tense, he replaced the box and walked to the window. Below, in the shadow of the rising moon, Saloma paced back and forth in front of the house. They both had secrets; he was sure of it. He was too ashamed to admit his shortcomings, and he was too proud to admit she was grieving motherhood. Both were facing challenges in their own way.

What he was certain of was that neither of them was turning to the one person who could guide their way. The Lord had always been a big part of their life together, but as of late, they had turned to their own understanding instead of the wisdom of *Gott*. Where had they gone wrong? But more importantly, how would he lead them back to where they needed to be before it was too late?

CHAPTER 8

Allie finished helping a customer at the counter just as the bell at the delivery door rang. Unlocking the double doors on the far end of the stock room revealed Saloma Raber.

Her uncle mentioned that someone from Raber Farms would be delivering apples that morning, and she was to set up a display once they arrived.

Unsure how to respond after their last encounter, Allie grabbed a cart and got busy unloading the crates of apples without so much as a word. It was Saloma who finally broke the silence.

"Do you have a check for me?"

"*Jah*, my uncle left one at the counter. I'll retrieve it as soon as I'm finished here."

Saloma skirted past her and into the store. Reasoning with herself, Allie thought. *Okay, don't make matters worse. Remember, be nice. Do I dare ask about Reuben again?*

She heard the woman holler as she stacked the last crates in the cold room. "Come on, girl, I don't have all day."

Just then, her uncle returned from errands and waved her away from the crates to help Mrs. Raber. "Go take care of her before she splits a seam." They both snickered at his comment, and Allie returned to the counter.

The air in the storeroom failed to move, and Allie opened the front door to let in a fresh breeze, just as Saloma busied herself with choosing a few greeting cards. Moving back behind the counter, Allie straightened up a small display of honey and asked. "How's Reuben these days?"

In a not-so-friendly reply, Saloma snorted. "Wouldn't know. Been gone for a few days now."

"Gone? Where to?"

"I'd say that's none of your business, *jah?*"

"Perhaps not. But I'm concerned he didn't tell me where he might go."

Before Allie could inquire more, her uncle stepped out from the stockroom and greeted Saloma. "The apples look wonderful. Already had a few inquiries about them this week. Three crates are already spoken for; I'm sure the other three will go quickly. Do you think you can deliver more tomorrow?"

"*Jah*, I'll send one of the boys by first thing."

The older woman headed toward the rack of hunting vests and beckoned her uncle to follow. "Tell me about these. Daniel has a birthday coming up, and I want only the best."

Saloma looked back over her shoulder, and Allie felt a surge of uneasiness at the woman's vindictive smile. *What is that all about?* She asked herself. Returning to stocking shelves, she lingered until Saloma carried her items to the counter before returning to the register. As she moved closer, her uncle directed her to finish what she was doing and told her he would take care of her.

"That will be twenty-four dollars." Her uncle stated. "Do you want to pay for it, or should I put it on your bill?"

"No, I'll take care of it today." The woman rummaged through her pocketbook. "That is if I can find my wallet. I was just at the bank, so I know it's here somewhere." Her voice raised an octave and pointed toward Allie. "It was her. I left my purse on the counter. There is no one else in the store. She must have taken it."

Allie's uncle was quick to defend her. "I'm sure Allie had nothing to do with it. Perhaps you left it in the cart?"

Her face flared. "I tell you, I had it when I came into the store."

"Allie, have you seen Mrs. Raber's wallet?"

There it was again; a daunting look in Saloma's eyes left Allie on edge as she moved toward the counter. As she moved things around and looked around the floor, she replied, "I haven't seen it. Are you sure you didn't leave it at the bank?"

Looking at her mockingly, Saloma said. "I'm not senile! I tell you it was in my purse when I arrived."

With a sudden urge to defend herself, she exclaimed. "Well, I didn't touch it."

Her glaring eyes slid and landed on Allie's bag, pointing with an accusing finger. "There. Check her bag. I bet she put it in there."

Allie reached for her bag and held it out. "Check it. I have nothing to hide."

With a look of apology, her uncle took the canvas tote. "This is ridiculous, Saloma. Allie would never..." His words stopped midair as he retrieved the black leather wallet from the top of Allie's bag.

"See. I told you it was her. You can bet I'll not let this pass. I'll be telling all my friends to shop elsewhere. If your employees can't be trusted, we have no business shopping here."

His glance grew sharper, and he quickly averted his scornful eyes and pleaded with Mrs. Raber. "Now, don't do anything hasty. I'll take care of this problem immediately; you can be sure of that. I'll not tolerate such behavior from my employees."

Abruptly, a wave of nausea encased Allie. It was like she was in a dream. Unable to form words, she could only stand by and watch the woman manipulate her uncle into believing the unspeakable. As Mrs. Raber turned to leave, a dangerous smile tipped her face. At that moment, Allie knew there was little hope she would ever have a future in Willow Springs or with Reuben Raber.

***

With no proof of her innocence, her uncle held little compassion for Allie's predicament. Whether he believed her story or not, Saloma was out to tarnish her name. All that concerned him was that the Rabers had clout, and Shetler's

Grocery would suffer financial hardship if he allowed her to continue to work there.

***

Sylvia was asleep in her chair when Allie got home, so she quietly retreated to her room. Unable to process what had happened without any friends to confide in, she pulled the covers over her head to drown out the daylight. She wept with fury, begging *Gott* to shed light on her actions to ward off such injustice. *Now what?* She thought. *I have no job, and my parents are in Africa. I'm sure I'll be asked to leave soon. Oh, Reuben, where are you?"*

When her tears tapered to sniffles, she brushed her wet hair off her cheek and crawled out of her cocoon. In a shifting gleam of sunlight, she followed it to the window. Across the yard, her aunt stood on her porch and gestured to her once she saw her in the window.

Lost in a sea of darkness, she forced her feet to follow her aunt's summons. Her eyes burned as she stepped out into the daylight, and she had to shield the brightness from penetrating the mounting pressure of new tears.

Her Aunt Leona had opened her home and her heart to Allie, and the thought of her thinking for one minute she could steal hurt her deeply. By the time she stepped into her aunt's open arms, her body racked with sobs. Through an array of hiccups, she appealed. "I...I promise...I...di...didn't ta...take...her wa...wallet.

Her aunt's loving arms pulled her closer. "*Shhh*...I know you didn't. But we must do what's best for the store."

Allie backed away, blew her nose, and sat on the step. Her aunt followed and wrapped an arm around her shoulders. "Why would she do something like this? I don't understand."

"Neither do we. Do you have any idea why she wouldn't want you here?"

Hot tears wet her throat, and she struggled to compose her thoughts. "I think she knows Reuben and I are seeing one another, and she doesn't like it."

"Reuben? Reuben Raber?

"I thought Virginia..."

Allie turned toward her. "What about Virginia?"

Shaking her head, she changed the subject. "Oh, it's nothing. I must have been mistaken. Anyways. You've been seeing

Reuben Raber. Isn't he a little old for you? What is he now? Twenty-three or so?"

"He's twenty-one." Allie hesitated and chose her words carefully. "Wasn't my *datt* twenty-one when he and my mom married? I think Mom was barely seventeen."

Her mother's sister smiled and tilted her head in a dreamy state. "*Oh*, your mother was so in love. It didn't matter that we were Amish, and your dad was Mennonite. They didn't let that stop them or the arrangements they made."

Leona held Allie's hand. "Perhaps history is repeating itself?"

Musing, Allie's voice turned sad. "I thought so. But I haven't heard from him in days. It's like he disappeared, and his mother won't tell me where he is. I just don't understand. This is so unlike him."

With a sense of reluctance, Leona asked, "Do you think he's having second thoughts?" She paused for a moment before continuing. "Maybe he's not willing to face so many obstacles."

"But we've talked about that and decided we could make it work. I even told him I would join his church if need be."

Leona shrugged her shoulders. "Maybe the problem doesn't lie with Reuben but the responsibilities he has to his family. He is the youngest and would be expected to care for his parents when that time comes." Leona met Allie's inquiring glare and continued. "Saloma's been known to be difficult."

"If that's the case, she's not even giving me a chance. And now that she's accused me of such lies, I'll never be able to prove to her I'm worthy."

Leona pulled in a breath and exhaled slowly. "Allie, you don't need to prove your worth to anyone. Especially Saloma Raber. Plus, we have no idea what's going on in her heart. Or why she feels threatened by you so much she would resort to such means."

Allie interrupted. "Lies, it's all a big lie. And I know she knows where Reuben is, but she won't tell me."

"Now, calm down. You may need to let it be right now. If *Gott* wants you and Reuben together, he will pave the way. I promise you, nothing Saloma can do will stand in his way."

"I really dislike her," Allie added.

Her aunt squeezed her hand. "Now, now, let's not justify one sin with another. We are to imitate Christ in our actions and thoughts. Even when it doesn't seem fair. Saloma is broken and struggling with something, and it's not for us to judge her."

"But…"

Leona held up her hand. "No, our hearts must settle on compassion, even for those who are hard to love."

A weary acceptance dropped over Allie as she wiped her nose with a tissue. "What am I supposed to do now? My parents are overseas, I have no job, and I don't know where Reuben is."

"Well, I have some of those questions figured out."

"I can go back to work?"

"No, I'm afraid that's not going to happen. But I've made a few phone calls and have a job waiting for you."

Allie tucked a wisp of hair behind her ear. "Where?"

"I have a cousin who runs a Coffee Café in Pinecraft, Florida who's always looking for good help. I tried calling her, but I've been unable to get anyone to answer. However, she called me a few days ago asking if I knew anyone who wanted to work for the winter. Seems they get swamped this time of year."

"Pinecraft? I couldn't go that far. What about Reuben? I can't just up and leave him with no word. He'll worry."

Her aunt's forehead creased in a question. "Maybe that's exactly what you need to do."

Allie rested her chin in her palms and pressed her elbows into her knees. "I just don't know. How can I leave until I find out what's going on with Reuben? What if he comes looking for me?"

"If he does, I'll tell him where he can find you."

"I guess I don't have much choice, do I?"

"No. I'm afraid not. Let Reuben figure out how to deal with whatever is going on with his mother. If it's *Gott's* will, he'll make it come to pass."

"But who will explain to Reuben what really happened? He'll only have his mother's side, not mine."

"Allie, we need to leave it in the Lord's hands. He's always working in a myriad of ways that we don't see. He may be doing something in Saloma's heart we know nothing about."

An unbearable anguish built up within Allie as she whispered, "I still don't like her much."

Leona wrapped her arm around Allie's shoulders and snickered. "I know, and you'll need to work through that with much prayer. But right now, you need to go pack your things. The Pioneer Trails bus leaves at two for Sarasota."

***

Sweat dripped off the tip of Reuben's nose as Elwin carried the last load of wet drywall from John's house. It had been days since the flood waters receded enough for them to return to access the damage. The air, laden with the smell of mildew, penetrated through the neighborhood. Large piles of debris littered both sides of the street.

Reuben wiped his forehead with the back of his arm. "Not sure I'll ever get used to this heat."

Elwin leaned on the fence and took a swig from a water bottle in his back pocket. "I like it. Just the thought of no snow sounds inviting. I'm thinking about staying."

"Not me," Reuben exclaimed. "I'm out of here as soon as I'm done helping John. I need to get back to Willow Springs."

Elwin straightened and nodded in the direction of Virginia walking toward them. "Fair game then, *jah?*"

Reuben grunted. "She's all yours."

Virginia waved and greeted them both. "Good day, *jah?*"

Elwin tossed his empty bottle in the trash. "Now that you're here, it is."

Rueben glanced sharply at his cousin as he headed back to the house. "Don't be long. We have work to do." He growled.

***

Virginia followed Reuben with her eyes. "What's his problem?"

"Who knows? He's been like that for days." Elwin leaned in closer and whispered, "I think it has something to do with what he left back in Willow Springs."

"Do you know who she is?" she asked in a curious tone.

Elwin's watchful head swiveled in Reuben's direction. "Not free to say, but I think it's pretty serious."

No matter how often she played his words and actions over in her head, Virginia couldn't believe there was no chance for their future. Reuben was all she'd hoped for, and she wasn't about to give up without a fight. When Reuben stopped and looked back toward them, she closed the gap between her and Elwin and laid her hand on his arm.

Startled when Elwin laid his hand on hers, she averted her eyes toward Elwin and suddenly was unnerved by his touch. As soon as Reuben headed back inside, she snatched her hand away and spat. "Don't get any ideas. I was just trying to get a reaction from Reuben."

Elwin thrust his face close. "I tell you; he's not drawn to you any longer. You're barking up the wrong tree if you think he is."

Her head dropped dejectedly. "I hope to change his mind." She looked up, pleading. "That is if I can employ your help some." Virginia continued to hold her breath as she observed Elwin pondering her words. The muggy air lay thick on his skin, pasting his dark hair to his neck, forcing him to wipe the moisture away. While he favored Reuben's lanky stature, there was a sense of mystery and rebellion in Elwin's eyes. It wasn't until his grin revealed a sudden rousing of attention that she asked, "So, would you be willing to help me win him back?"

"What do you have in mind?"

Her conscience piqued slightly, but she pushed it aside to say, "I thought perhaps you could pretend to show interest in me."

He didn't say a word but continued to ponder her request. A hard knot formed in her stomach, and for an instant, she doubted her plan would work. That was, until he raised an eyebrow and smiled most deviously. "I wouldn't need to play-act."

What was it she saw in his face that made her insides churn? Was it apprehension or excitement? She let out a small gasp, then replied, "As long as you know my attention is merely to win Reuben back."

He reached down and tugged on her *kapp* string. "As long as you know I'm not playacting."

He turned and walked away, leaving remnants of his overpowering presence. *What have I done?* She thought. Nervous but somewhat compelled by his statement, she mumbled to herself. "A little too flirty for my liking." She paused to watch him disappear behind the house and thought. *Or is he?*

***

Elwin smiled as he sauntered away. He felt Virginia's eyes bore into his back, but he refused to turn around. *Two can play this game*, he thought. He knew there was no way she'd win Reuben back, but he'd undoubtedly enjoy partaking in her cunning proposal. While he found Virginia most appealing, what intrigued him the most was her passion for going after what she wanted.

He peered around the side of the house and watched her walk away. Trying not to dampen his enthusiasm, he chastised himself for agreeing to help. Was this the way he really wanted to win her heart? How could he convince her to take him seriously if their time together was based on a lie? Keeping out of view, he kicked a stone and devised his own plan. One that would show Virginia that he was worthy of his true intentions.

CHAPTER 9

Allie leaned her head against the cool window and closed her eyes. The constant motion of the bus and the overwhelming odor of exhaust left her stomach rolling. Leaving Willow Springs without knowing why Reuben hadn't gotten word to her left her reeling in grief. Her mind was racing with what could have happened or what she might have done to make him change his mind so suddenly. If it weren't for the older woman who sat next to her keeping her company, she may have cried herself to sleep.

In a honey toned voice, the woman asked, "Are you going to help with cleanup? My daughter and son-in-law live on Fry Street and said their home was spared but many of their neighbors suffered water damage."

"Cleanup?"

"Haven't you heard? Hurricane Frances hit the Gulf Coast right around Siesta Key last week. Most of us are going to Pinecraft to help with the cleanup."

"That must be why my aunt couldn't get her cousin on the phone. She tried for days."

"*Jah*, if she doesn't have a cell phone, there would be no way of reaching her. Phone service and power is out all over Sarasota County. It will be a month or more before it's restored."

"I'm supposed to be going for a job at the Coffee Café. I hope my trip isn't wasted."

The elderly woman's faint smile showed satisfaction. "I highly doubt that. If the café has damage, they'll need plenty of hands and yours won't go to waste. Where are you staying?"

An anxious feeling moved up to Allie's throat. "I'm not sure. My aunt assures me her cousin will put me up." She pulled a small slip of paper from her pocket. "She lives on Gilbert Street."

"*Jah*, that's not too far from my daughter's." The woman studied the address. "I think that's right next to John Raber." She handed the slip of paper across the aisle to her friend. "I think you're correct. That's John from Raber's Furniture. He makes the finest tables…"

Allie tuned the women out as they continued to talk about Raber's Furniture. A smile on Reuben's face came to her mind as she recalled a conversation, they had had a few weeks earlier.

"I aspire to be as good as my Uncle John someday. He makes the finest furniture in all of Florida and if he were closer, I wouldn't think twice about working with him."

Allie gazed out the window and continued to remember how Reuben dreamed about being a sought-after craftsman like his uncle.

"Why not?"

"Why not what?" he asked.

"Go work for him. What's stopping you? If he's that good, I think you would benefit from working under him."

Reuben shrugged his shoulders. "Florida is so far away. And besides, I'm not sure I'd enjoy the heat. Some say it can get over one-hundred degrees in the summertime."

"The adventure of a new place sounds exciting to me. Don't you ever want to experience life in other areas?"

"Can't say I have." His smile widened. "I'm content in Willow Springs."

With a deep heaviness, she closed her eyes and prayed. *Lord, wherever Reuben is, keep him safe and lead him back to me…*

***

Reuben looked through a stack of books. "Uncle John, do you have an address directory for Lawrence County? I need to call Shetler's Grocery."

John pointed toward the cupboard near the kitchen sink. "I think so. I keep it over there. It's old, but I doubt they've changed their number."

With Elwin's cell phone finally at full charge, he was determined to find a way to reach Allie. She must be worried sick, and he scolded himself for not calling sooner. She typically stayed after closing to clean up, and he prayed she'd be available to talk to him.

He took a hopeful breath as the phone rang.

"Hello, Shetler's Grocery."

"Mrs. Shetler?"

"*Jah*, this is Leona Shetler. How can I help you?"

"I'm looking to speak with Allie. Is she available?"

A long pause filled the dead space as he expected her answer.

"Allie? No, I'm sorry she doesn't work here anymore. Is there something I can help you with?"

As if he'd been kicked in the ribs by a mule, he wheezed. "What do you mean she doesn't work there? Where did she go?"

"Reuben Raber, is that you?"

"*Jah.*"

"I'm sorry Reuben, but we had to let Allie go. She tried to see you before she left, but your mother..."

"My mother what?" he interrupted.

"Well...she wouldn't let Allie see you."

The muscles in Reuben's jaw twitched. "Did she tell her I had to leave to help my uncle in Pinecraft?"

He heard the woman giggle on the other end. "Did you say Pinecraft?"

"*Jah.* My uncle needed my help in his furniture shop. But Hurricane Frances hit as soon as I got here, and I've been dealing with that and haven't had a minute to call. I sent her a note before I left. Do you know if she received it?"

"*Nee,* I don't think so. She was quite upset that she hadn't heard from you."

"Can you tell me where Allie is?" he asked tensely.

The woman's voice took a sense of excitement. "She's arriving on the two o'clock bus."

"Here in Pinecraft?"

"*Jah*, in Pinecraft."

"Does she know I'm here?'

"*Nee*, and I'll let her explain why when she arrives." The woman paused for a moment before continuing. "It's not my story to tell."

Reuben ended the call and leaned on the counter, looking toward Elwin.

"Allie's on her way here."

Elwin laughed. "And the plot thickens."

"What's that supposed to mean?"

He grinned. "Nothing that won't work its way out in my favor."

Reuben glared at him with unsure eyes. "What are you up to this time?"

"Trust me, the ball just fell in my court."

"I don't like that look. You're up to something. What is it?"

Elwin stood, slapped him on the back and headed out the door hollering, "I've got you covered."

Reuben frowned in annoyance. Elwin was up to no good, for sure and certain.

***

Precisely at two o'clock, the bus pulled into the lot at the Tourist Mennonite Church on Bahia Vista Street. For the last thirty minutes, Allie agonized over the destruction she witnessed throughout Sarasota County. Piles of debris, damaged homes, and overturned vehicles lined the streets. An overwhelming sense of dread landed on her chest as she wondered what she was walking into. She wasn't even sure where she was staying or if she had a job waiting for her.

As she stepped off the bus, she shielded her eyes from the afternoon sun and moved to the side of the bus to await her bag. The salty air stuck to her skin as she asked her seatmate, "I have no idea where I'm going. Will you point me in the direction of Gilbert Street?"

Just as the woman started to rattle off instructions, she felt a hand on her shoulder. Turning toward the pressure and focusing on Reuben's face through the sun took a moment.

Without hesitation, she engulfed him in a hug. "Reuben!"

Sensing his uncomfortable state at her public show of affection, she stepped back quickly. "What are you doing here, and how did you know I was coming?"

He took her bag as the driver handed it to her, guiding her away from the crowd. "I called the store looking for you, and your aunt told me where I could find you."

"Have you been in Pinecraft all this time? Why didn't you tell me where you were going?"

"I did. I put a note in the mail on my way out of town." He paused and grumbled, "I'm certain my *mamm* intercepted it somehow."

Without realizing it, her face turned to a scowl at the mention of his mother and Reuben asked, "What did she do now?"

Allie didn't want to put a wedge between Reuben and his mother, but he had to know what she was accusing her of before it got back to him. Heaven knows the Amish grapevine works fast. Even if she was a thousand miles away.

After leading him to a table outside the Coffee Café across the street, she proceeded to explain to him why she was fired and forced to come to Florida.

Obviously irritated, he hung his head and apologized. "I don't even know what to say. She's gone too far this time."

Lowering her voice and laying her hand over his, she whispered, "I promise you I didn't take her wallet. She must have placed it in my bag when I had my back turned."

His hands clutched hers. "I have no doubt that's exactly what she did. She has been against us seeing one another from the start."

"But why? I don't understand what she has against me."

"Who knows what goes on in her head? I think she thinks she's losing me, and you'll keep me from joining the Amish church."

"But we already discussed that. I told you I'd join the Amish church if you felt that was best for us."

"I know, but I haven't told her. I didn't feel it was any of her business."

Allie sighed. "Now what? How can we move forward with our plans if we don't have her blessing?"

Reuben leaned his elbows on his knees and wrung his hands together. After a few moments, he sat up and declared, "We'll get married here."

Allie sucked in a breath. "Are you sure?"

"Why not? You love me, right? And I love you. What's stopping us?"

She thought for a moment. "The only thing that's stopping us is I won't be eighteen for another three weeks."

"Perfect, that's about how long Uncle John thinks it will take to get his orders caught up. In the meantime, we can find a place to live, and I can prove to my uncle that I'd make a great employee. Then maybe he'll hire me on permanently."

"So, we'll stay in Florida?"

His eyes sparkled, as he asked, "That is if you like it here. It's hot and crowded this time of year, but I think you might enjoy it." He hesitated and anticipated her reply.

She looked toward Bahia Vista Street and then back at the neighborhood behind them. "As long as I'm with you, I can make anywhere work."

He squeezed her hand and smiled just as Elwin and Virginia ambled up behind them.

***

Virginia knew the minute she spotted Reuben sitting next to Allie. He had always been true to their no touch rule outlined by the *Ordnung*, but by the way he was huddled in close, she sensed his intentions. A piece of her heart broke away as she gulped for a breath. She looked up at Elwin. "Allie Mast?"

"*Jah*, I told you your plan wouldn't work."

"Why didn't you tell me?"

He gave her a callous shrug. "Figured you'd find out soon enough."

It took all she had to approach them without baring her soul. In a matter of seconds, all her hopes and dreams faded away, replaced by the image of Reuben's soft eyes as he looked at Allie. She forced her feet to continue to move and thought. *Mamm always said you could read a man's heart through his eyes.* She swallowed hard when she realized Reuben had never looked at her in the same manner.

"Allie?" Virginia called with an emptiness in her voice.

"Virginia, what are you doing here?"

"I came to visit my *grossmommi*. And you?"

"I start a new job at the Coffee Café soon."

"Who's helping Leona at the store?"

"No one right now."

"Oh my! What happened?"

Allie looked over at Reuben and shrugged. "It's a long story and one I'd prefer not to get into."

The conversation died for a few moments as she looked over at Reuben. It was like they shared a secret language without any words and at that moment, she knew for certain what he'd been trying to tell her for days. When she restored her focus back to Elwin, he sent a sly smile.

She hesitated, choosing her words carefully. "Reuben, may I speak with you privately?"

He stood and leaned down to whisper in Allie's ear. "We stepped out for a few years. I'm sure she wants to wish us well." He lingered, allowing his words to sink in before following Virginia to the other side of the patio.

Reuben braced himself as her questions came like an inquisition.

"Why didn't you tell me you were seeing Allie? Don't you think I deserved to know? Just how long has this been going on?"

Her questions came flying fast, leaving him little room to answer. "Does it really matter now?"

"Matter?" she spat. "Of course it matters. I've been making a fool of myself for days now." Her voice trailed off, and she slumped in a nearby chair. "If only I'd known it was Allie; I wouldn't have pressed you so hard."

He tried to offer a sincere apology. "I tried to tell you I moved on."

"That's the problem," she said soberly. "I didn't. I prayed you'd come back."

Reuben sat next to her. "I didn't mean to hurt you."

She looked tenderly at him. "Are you sure Allie is the one?"

He glanced back over to where Elwin and Allie were sitting. "I've never been so sure of anything else."

"Your mother isn't going to make it easy for her."

"*Jah*, I know, and she's already proving to be a challenge."

"What are you going to do?"

He stood. "I'm going to make it where she has no choice but to accept Allie into the family."

"How so?"

With a sudden flood of emotion, he stated, "I'm going to make her my *fraa*."

***

Allie couldn't help but quiz Elwin. "Did they see each other for long?"

"Longer than I've ever stepped out with someone."

"What happened?"

He looked faintly amused. "You."

"I feel bad. I've talked to Virginia about Reuben." She paused. "But I don't think I've ever mentioned him by name."

His grin widened. "All I know is she's open game now."

"Elwin! That's a crude way to look at things."

"Well, it's true. Now that she sees he's not changing his mind, maybe she'll pay me some attention."

An ironic smile touched her lips. "You sweet on her?" Allie elbowed him. "Perhaps I can help."

"How so?"

"You just let me worry about that." She lifted her voice in a serious tone. "All I ask is you keep the rude remarks to yourself. No girl wants to hear such things."

With a guttural sound, he replied, "It's not like she doesn't know how I am. We went to school together forever."

"Yeah, but this is different. If you want her to take you seriously, you need to put your best foot forward. Show her you can act like an adult and not a silly teenager."

"Hey…wait a minute, I'm a man."

She mocked him with laughter. "Then act like one."

They stopped talking when Reuben and Virginia returned to the table.

Reuben picked up Allie's bag. "We best go figure out if you have a place to stay."

Virginia locked her arm in Allie's. "My *grossmommi* has an extra bedroom. Why don't you stay with me?"

Allie met her words with an inquiring gaze. "You're not upset with me?"

"Upset? No. Disappointed, *jah*." Virginia smiled toward Reuben. "If I can't have him, then at least my best friend can."

Tracy Fredrychowski

CHAPTER 10

Allie and Reuben strode along the path beside Phillippi Creek under a canopy of mature oak trees shading them from the hot Florida sun. It had been over a month since she arrived, and they had settled into a comfortable routine. Hurricane cleanup was just about complete, and Reuben was now working at his uncle's furniture shop and she at the Coffee Café. Reuben took her hand and guided her to a bench overlooking the shuffleboard courts.

"I've been so busy at work we haven't had much time to discuss things."

With a slight nod and a tentative smile, she asked, "What do we need to talk about?" She didn't doubt what he was referring to by the longing in his eyes.

"I have Friday off. Would you like to get married?"

Her face flushed, and with starry eyes replied, "I'd like nothing more." She hesitated momentarily before asking, "Are you sure you want to do it this way? Without family or your community around."

He wrapped his arm around her shoulders and pulled her close, kissing her head. "I don't need any of that. I only need you."

He lifted her chin and lightly kissed her lips. At that moment, it didn't matter that his mother wouldn't approve or that her family wouldn't be there. All that mattered was *Gott* had given her the man of her dreams.

***

All morning, Daniel studied the pile of invoices and ledgers in his office. No matter how he looked at it, there was no way out of his current predicament. He turned his eyes to the note that showed up under his office door that morning. His shame grew as the threats and warnings were becoming more frequent.

When Almer's voice echoed over the notions whirling through his head, he followed the angry sound to the storage barn. Just as he stepped inside, a wagon piled high with crates of apples broke a wheel and slid backward, pinning him against the wall.

Within seconds, the pain in his right leg was unbearable, and he yelled in agony. The tear in his joint and the snap of bone rebounded as it cut through his skin. Heat like he'd never experienced before tore through his leg like knives. A flurry of activity surrounded him as he reached for Almer's hand, just as darkness took over.

Saloma took a cake out of the oven as Almer barreled through the back door. "*Mamm*, go to the phone shanty and call for help. *Datt's* hurt!"

Within ten minutes, a screech of sirens sounded from the fire department two miles away.

Saloma sat at Daniel's side, holding his hand as the boys removed the wagon and apple crates that engulfed him. Fading in and out of consciousness, his eyes momentarily went wide with fear as he murmured, "Lock the office."

Brushing off his strange request, Saloma barked orders in a panic. "Hurry, make a path for the firemen!" Her breath caught in her throat as she noticed the pool of blood under Daniel's leg and the unnatural position of his femur as they uncovered him.

Almer propped his *datt's* head under a folded jacket and applied pressure to his leg to stop the bleeding. Saloma hissed, "How did this happen?"

Her accusing tone landed heavily, and Almer's reply turned blood cold as he growled. "It was an accident!"

"You boys are careless; look what it's cost your *datt*."

Daniel squeezed her hand and murmured, "Stop."

Saloma lifted her head as the emergency medical technician rolled a stretcher into the barn. Within seconds, they asked her to step aside and began asking Almer a series of questions as they stabilized Daniel. Terror sprung up in Saloma's throat as she watched the scene unfold. Daniel took on an ashen color as the paramedic started an IV and instructed the EMT to apply more pressure to the femoral artery.

Gasping at the reality, an older firefighter pulled her aside. "Ma'am, I assume you're his wife."

"*Jah*."

He continued to ask her questions until they stabilized him enough to move him to the stretcher. An eerie moan filled the barn as Daniel cried out. The mere sound forced Saloma's belly to tighten. She moved to his side as they approached the waiting ambulance. As the EMTs prepared to secure his stretcher inside, they stopped long enough so she could bend to speak to him.

"Hold tight, my love."

Daniel's eyes flickered open, and he made his request once again. "Lock the office."

The hairs along the nape of her neck prickled at his strange plea. "Okay," she whispered.

The paramedic instructed the EMT and then asked her, "Would you like to ride with him?"

Daniel grabbed her hand. "*Nee*...office."

Her emotions were chaotic, and she signaled to Almer. "Come, go with your *datt*. I must take care of something."

Confused by her request, he balked. "What could be more important than this?"

"Now's not the time to ask questions; just go!"

Saloma stood unemotional for a few moments as the ambulance pulled away. She instructed one of the younger boys to call for a driver and headed to Daniel's office.

On the verge of hysteria, she couldn't imagine what was so important that he insisted she not go with him. As she opened the door, a few papers blew off his desk. As she bent to retrieve them, the shocking words in one of the letters forced her to fall into the chair.

Mr. Raber,

This is our third attempt to collect on your outstanding debt. As our contract outlines, if payment is not made by December 31st, we will take immediate possession of Raber Farms and its two hundred acres. All houses, buildings, and orchards will become the property of Mercer Lending and will be sold accordingly.

Sincerely,

Johnathan Mercer, Chief Lending Officer

Saloma shuddered in a breath and continued to read through the stack. All said much of the same except for a handwritten note with a strange but terrifying message.

This is your last chance. Meet me at noon at the covered bridge. Life as you know it is at stake. Don't take this warning lightly and bring the box...I know you have it.

A spasm of fear gripped Saloma's heart. "What on earth have you done?" she mumbled. Sifting through the stack of invoices, she trembled at how dire things had gotten. As far as she could tell, they had been struggling for some time. Daniel mortgaged the farm repeatedly, and the outstanding fuel and equipment repairs invoices outweighed anything they made from selling apples. She even discovered he'd sold farm shares to their competitor, Curtman's Apple Orchard and Cider Mill. "How could you?" She moaned.

Resting her eyes, she prayed, *Lord, what am I to do with all this? Why now, Lord, why?"*

She didn't know how long she stayed in that position, crying out all while going through every scenario in her head, from releasing it to the lending company to meeting whoever demanded payment at noon. No clear direction came. Instead, a deep-seated dread settled on her shoulders. Was this her punishment for accusing Allie? Or perhaps it was *Gott's* way of showing her how wrong she was in threatening to expose Bishop Weaver's family secret.

The distant sound of an approaching buggy shook her from her self-absorbed trance. Scooping the stack of papers off the desk and putting them into a drawer, she quickly moved to the door, locking it behind her.

Mose Weaver stopped just short of where she stood, and a van pulled up behind them. "I passed an ambulance; what happened?"

"Daniel got pinned behind a wagon. " Lost in thought, she noted the noon sun and wondered what she might do about the note.

"Saloma? Did you hear me?"

Startled at the bishop's pitch, she replied, "*Jah*, his leg is broken, and by the puddle of blood in the barn, he lost a good bit."

The boys hollered to her as they climbed into the van. "I've got to go. Did you need something?"

"*Nee*, not with you." He paused for a moment and then stated. "Daniel and I had business to contend with."

His emphasis on *'business'* made her wonder if the bishop knew the state of their affairs. "He won't be up for any business dealing anytime soon. I'll take care of things when I return home."

Mose patted the journal in his shirt pocket. "Not likely."

Her trembling subsided long enough to watch him pull away as a fresh wave of anger crept in. His smugness left her reeling as she tried to figure out how to get her hands on his precious notebook.

Following the boys in the van, she clicked on her seatbelt and stared out the window as she worried about Daniel and the farm. As they crossed Willow Creek, her eyes followed the water toward the covered bridge. Wishing their path would take them to the bridge, she sighed as the driver turned in the opposite direction. She wondered if whoever was to meet Daniel was waiting and what would happen if he didn't appear.

She leaned her head on the cool window and closed her eyes. Fresh tears brimmed her bottom eyelashes as she recalled Daniel's dismal state. Not wanting to admit she was to blame for their recent misfortune, she opened her eyes and started to badger the boys about their negligence again.

When all sat in silence, refusing to engage in her outburst, she huffed out a long sigh, wrung her hands, and rubbed the numbness from her fingers. Her boys were no strangers to her rants, and they learned early on to let her go on until she numbed her hurtful tongue. Suddenly, a familiar tension arose, and a headache matured.

***

Allie followed Reuben up two flights of stairs to the upstairs apartment. The narrow hallway was dark and gloomy, but sunlight filtered into the small space as soon as Reuben unlocked the door.

Reuben examined the exterior of the two modest rooms, flipped on every switch, and checked out every nook and cranny. "I'm not sure about this. It's so cramped here. How can I ask you to live like this?"

Allie smiled as if she was holding onto a beautiful secret. "It's perfect." She ran her hand over the counter, opened the refrigerator, and checked every cupboard. "There's plenty of space. Besides, it's just you and me. What more do we need?"

Reuben stood at the window. "We don't even have a yard."

Allie came up behind him and wrapped her arm around his middle. "We don't need a yard; we have a park across the street."

"I'm not sure, Allie. Bahia Vista Street is so busy. The noise will keep us up at night." He struggled to open the window. When it finally released its hold from the swollen wood, he exclaimed, "You'd never be able to open these yourself."

She giggled. "I doubt we'd need to with the air conditioning."

Reuben sighed. "I didn't think we'd use it."

His comment made her face drain of color. "Not use the A/C? Don't you think it'll get too hot? We're on the second floor and in Florida, I'd say we won't have much choice in the matter."

Allie moved back into the tiny kitchen, opened the microwave, and admired the small electric stove. "Everything here runs by electricity. Not sure they have propane or wood-powered anything in Florida."

Reuben leaned on the wall and crossed his arms over his chest. "It fits in our budget, but it's not how I envisioned our life together."

Allie sighed. "We've looked at three places now, and you've found fault with each one. What are you looking for?"

"Something a bit simpler. All have too much of the *Englisch* world. We don't need all that fuss. How can we keep our eyes focused on the Lord with so many distractions?"

Opening the apartment-sized oven, she replied, "But think of all the yummy desserts I can make for you. Just because they all come with modern conveniences doesn't mean we must use them."

"That's what you say now. But I'm afraid we'll get accustomed to the ease of things and forget what matters."

Allie moved to Reuben's side and looped her arm in his. "How about you tell me what the perfect place would be?"

He placed his hand over hers. "I don't know. Maybe a small one-story *haus* with a big front porch that overlooked green space. Maybe a quiet street where we could hear the birds."

She laughed. "What you're describing sounds like something in Willow Springs."

He guided her to the door. "Let's go. This place isn't right for us."

With an inner sigh, she followed him down the stairs, saying goodbye to yet another perfect apartment. Reuben's mood continued to sink with each passing day since they got married three days ago. She was beginning to think Florida wasn't what Reuben had in mind.

They both remained silent as they strolled the eight blocks back to Pinecraft. Instead of heading back to Uncle John's, Reuben led them down Carter Avenue and into Pinecraft Park. After locating a free bench under a large pin oak, he muttered, "I think we need to talk."

Allie knew all but too well when he got extra quiet; he thought deeply about something. His mouth began to twitch slightly at one corner. "I'm not sure Florida is right for us."

She gave a faint nod. "Okay. What is?"

Reuben leaned his elbows on his knees, picked up a loose twig, and rolled it between his fingers. "Some place less busy." He hesitated for a few moments. "It's just so noisy here, and I'm not sure I can handle the heat in the summertime."

She watched him, unblinking, and asked, "Are you thinking about moving back to Willow Springs?"

"*Nee.* We can go to Sugarcreek if you want."

Allie took a few minutes to absorb his request before responding. "It would be nice to be near my parents when they're in town."

Something more was weighing on Reuben's mind, and she didn't rush him as he gathered his thoughts. "I thought I could make it work here, but I'd prefer someplace cooler."

With a small, prim smile, she leaned in closer. "I told you before I can make any place work as long as I'm with you. And while I'm not so sure moving back to Willow Springs would be wise…with your mother and all, I'll go wherever you take us and be content."

He snorted a deep laugh. "*Jah*, I agree about my mother. Then Sugarcreek it is?"

"If that's where you'll be happy, then that's where we'll go." She squeezed his arm. "So, when do we leave?"

"It would be perfect if we could get Elwin to drive us back, but it looks like he and Virginia have hit it off and are content to make Pinecraft something permanent. So, we must look at the bus schedule and see when we can head back."

"Will John be upset you're leaving?"

"*Nee*, he knows how I feel about Florida. And I'm sure he'll give me a good recommendation. I can't imagine having trouble finding a job in Sugarcreek."

"I can get my old job back at the diner to help out."

"You'll do no such thing," he said with a smile. "You'll have enough to do keeping house and tending to the garden."

"We'll have a garden?"

He looked at her quizzically. "If you want one?"

"I've never gardened before, but I'll try if you think it's important."

His eyebrows shot up. "We'll need to fill the cellar for the winter, *jah*?"

Embarrassed she hadn't thought it essential, she stumbled over her words in agreement. "*Jah*...I suppose so."

She tried hard to hide her disappointment in not staying in Pinecraft and enjoying more liberties than Reuben's upbringing allowed. However, she could tell he felt strongly about returning to a simpler lifestyle, and she would follow his lead no matter what. Even if it meant returning to a more conservative way of life than what she was accustomed to. Their differences were starting to show themselves increasingly with each passing day.

They heard Virginia and Elwin call out to them as they moved their way from the other side of the shuffleboard court.

Elwin hollered. "We've been looking for you. Almer's been trying to reach you."

"Almer? Why?"

"Seems your *datt* had an accident, and you're to come home at once."

Standing at Elwin's comment, Reuben asked, "Serious?"

"Bad enough that he's in the hospital, and you're being beckoned home."

Allie grabbed his arm. "We have no idea what the bus schedule is. How will we get home fast?"

Elwin looked over at Virginia. "We were planning on returning to Willow Springs, so we'll just have to move it up some."

"Good thing you just got the truck fixed, but all of us in the front of your box truck? Won't that be tight?"

Elwin nudged Virginia's shoulder. "We don't mind sitting close, *jah*?"

Virginia slapped his arm. "I'll tolerate it if I must if you promise to behave yourself," she joked.

Allie smiled at her friend, who had clearly taken a liking to Elwin's colorful personality. He was a little too much for her to handle, but Virginia had a way of keeping him in line.

Reuben's eyes grew somber as he turned back toward Allie. "I guess our plans are changing once again."

She answered wryly, hoping to hide her apprehension about facing his mother. What would she do when she found out they were married? With any luck, she would be too concerned with Daniel to care. "*Jah,* I'd say so."

CHAPTER 11

A fury of activity surrounded Saloma as she prepared the downstairs bedroom for Daniel. Two of the boys volunteered to bring their father home while she set things up for his long recovery.

Glancing at the clock, she finished making the bed and headed outside to Daniel's office. She barely had time to think over the last few days, so she wanted to look for whatever box the mysterious note spoke of while by herself. She was confident its contents would give her more clues into what her husband had gotten himself into.

Before she made her way across the yard, Reuben and Elwin pulled up to the *haus*. Relief flooded her as Elwin and Virginia stepped out. Looking over their shoulders, she watched Reuben and Allie appear hand in hand around the front of the truck. Her blood boiled, and she hissed, "What is she doing here?"

Reuben's face took on a stern expression, but Allie spoke up. "Mrs. Raber, I'm not sure what I've done to upset you, but as Reuben's wife, I have as much right to be here as he."

"*Fraa?*" Saloma began to shake and thrust her words at Rueben. "How could you? I won't have it. I won't have you giving up your heritage for a silly summer romance. No sense, I tell you. No sense at all!"

Saloma turned toward Virginia. "I thought you were going with him to Florida to prevent this from happening. This is not what we talked about." Waving them off, she pushed through them, heading to the barn, leaving a trail of verbal disappointment on her way. "The whole mess of you are crazy. I don't have time for any of you. And you can bet you've not heard the last of this one. I'll be taking this to the bishop for sure and certain."

In shock, Allie stood in utter disbelief. The look on Reuben's face was disheartening, almost like he was upset with her. "I'm sorry; I shouldn't have blurted it out like that."

His voice had an edge of irritation. "Regarding my mother, it's best you let me handle things."

Mortified he'd reprimanded her in front of Virginia and Elwin, she fought to control the lump that had lodged into her throat, preventing her from responding.

A ripple of uneasiness settled in her chest as he instructed Elwin. "We'll be staying at the *doddi haus*. Please leave our bags on the front porch."

Reuben's eyes softened a bit when he turned back to her. "Wait for me there. No one has lived there in a while, so it might need to be cleaned up some."

Feeling like she'd been sent away for bad behavior; she followed Elwin back to the truck.

Virginia ambled beside her. "Don't worry about Saloma. She'll come around when she sees how much Reuben loves you, and besides, she just likes getting her own way."

Allie gave Virginia a sideways glance and asked, "What did you and Mrs. Raber have planned?"

Virginia looped her arm through hers and whispered, "It doesn't matter now because I would never dream of coming between you and Reuben." She nodded in Elwin's direction. "Besides, I have my eyes set on someone else these days."

"Why do you think she dislikes me so?"

Virginia shrugged. "All I know is she's afraid Reuben won't join the church. She's unhappy with your different backgrounds and fears it will take him away from his family."

Allie stiffened and squared her shoulders. "What she should be more afraid of is me. If she thinks she's coming between my husband and me, she has another think coming. Doesn't she realize a man is supposed to cleave to his wife and not his mother?"

Virginia giggled. "If anyone can keep that woman in line, it will be you."

Picking up her bag, Allie exclaimed, "I let her get away with blaming me for stealing her wallet; I'm not going to let her get away with putting strife in my marriage."

"I still can't believe she would stoop so low." Virginia held her hand up. "I take that back. I can imagine it. She's ruthless and needs someone like you to put her in her place." Virginia shook her head. "You'll have your hands full. Are you sure you're up for it?"

Allie opened the front door to the *doddi haus* and exclaimed, "Do I have a choice? When you marry, you get a spouse and wed his whole family. The good, the bad, and, unfortunately, the ugly."

Virginia smiled and patted her on the shoulder. "I'll pray *Gott* gives you a heart of compassion when it comes to Saloma Raber."

"It will take more than prayer. It will take setting up boundaries we both can live with."

Allie waved from the porch as Elwin and Virginia drove away. As she turned back inside, she stood in the doorway and offered a prayer. *Lord, I'm unsure what to do about Saloma, but I trust you do. Please help me bind my words and help me not to react with emotion but to show love and mercy in all circumstances. I can't see all you see and want to believe that you are working this out for good. Lord, give me the same loving patience for Saloma that you show toward me. Amen*

***

Reuben's voice bore a trace of threat. "I won't have you speaking to Allie that way. Whether you like it or not, she's my *fraa*, and I expect you to treat her like part of the family."

Saloma's face reddened. "Family? You didn't consider your family when you ran off and got married without letting us know. What will the bishop say? He'll never consent to you joining the church after this escapade."

Taking a profound breath, Reuben tried calming his racing heart to deal with his mother the only way he knew how. "Would you have accepted her if I did the things the right way?"

"Of course not," she snapped. "She's not Amish, which will put a wedge in your future."

"You're not making sense. What difference does it make? We're still going to join an Amish church. She knows how important that is to me and has agreed."

Reuben watched as his mother seemed to calm slightly with his declaration before she included, "It won't work. She'll tire of simple living and convince you to live a more worldly life."

"*Mamm,* what difference does it make if we follow the Amish church or perhaps one day choose a more liberal Mennonite church?"

"See! Exactly what I mean. She's already put that thought in your head."

"She's done no such thing."

Saloma shuffled papers in a pile and paused briefly before asking, "Did you come home to help?"

"*Jah*, I suppose I did. At least until *Datt* gets back on his feet that is. Then perhaps I'll go back and work for Byler's Furniture."

He watched as his mother's face took on an edge of worry. "It's a mess. We're in dire need of a miracle, and we'll need all the help we can get."

"What's a mess?"

Saloma rolled her hands in the air over the papers strewed across the desk. "This. All of this. There are bills, bills, and more bills, and no way to pay them all. We'll be forced to close if we don't devise a way to dig ourselves out of this financial disarray."

"The farm is financially strapped?"

"More than that. On the verge of foreclosure as far as I can tell."

"Do Almer and the other boys know?"

"*Jah*, we've all been trying to find a way out of it."

Saloma pushed the note across the desk. "I found this the other day. I'm afraid your father has gotten into something fishy. I've searched everywhere for a box, hoping it would shed some light on what he's been hiding."

"Have you asked him about it?"

"*Nee*, he's been in so much pain I didn't want to burden him. Reuben, I'm concerned. I haven't shared that note with the others or the fact that when I came home from the hospital the other night, someone had been in the *haus*. As far as I could tell, nothing was stolen, but they were looking for something."

Reuben took a few seconds to read the note again. "What do you think it could be?"

With a grave sigh, his mother slumped back in the chair. "Your guess is as good as mine. Your father has kept this from me for the last six months. He only shared it with us last week."

Reuben handed the note back. "I think we should talk to *Datt* about it when he's feeling better. I'm sure he'll have a good explanation."

"I pray he does," Saloma whined as she rubbed the numbness out of her arm.

Reuben studied his mother for a moment. "*Mamm,* you don't look well."

She rubbed her arm and then moved to the back of her neck. "I must have a pinched nerve or something in my neck. My arm and hand are numb, and I have been having headaches." She rolled her shoulders and then stood, steadying herself when a wave of dizziness made her lose her balance. "I'm sure it's nothing Dr. Smithson can't tend to. I'll see him as soon as we get your *datt* settled."

Reuben reached out to steady her. "You won't be much help to *datt* if you don't care for yourself."

She shooed his hand away. "It's the last thing I need to worry about right now. Your *datt* and this farm are more important."

"Allie and I can help, so don't think you need to do it alone."

Without warning, his mother flailed him with unkind words about the woman he loved. He felt betrayed by her outlandish behavior, and he wondered how to protect Allie.

"I don't need her help. I'm plenty capable of taking care of things without her involvement."

Reuben raised his voice. "What is it you have against her? You haven't even given her a try."

She held her hand up. "I don't have the time or energy for this right now. Just know I'm not going to let this stand." Her words hung between them, flat and final, but she continued to add, "Don't think for one minute you'll be staying on the farm."

"I figured we'd stay in the *doddi haus*."

"You'll do no such thing."

"*Mamm,* you're being unreasonable."

"Unreasonable is you bringing that girl into this family."

Reuben's jaw clenched before he snapped, "Enough! This is my life, and Allie is part of it whether you like it or not. So, you best start warming up to the idea."

His mother stormed past him, grumbling a rebuttal. "I won't do it. She'll never be welcomed in my home."

A heaviness hovered over Reuben as he watched her stomp away. He lowered himself into his father's chair, unwilling to continue defending Allie to his mother and not ready to tell his new *fraa* what she was up against. As he rearranged the stack of invoices, he knocked over a mug of pens to the floor. Moving to pick them up, he noticed a hidden folder taped to the underside of the desk.

Reuben groaned as he read the terms of the high-interest loan that bore his father's signature. In the margin and in his father's handwriting, the words *BAIT & SWITCH SCHEME* were clearly printed. He didn't know much about the financial industry, but he knew enough that what his father had agreed to went against everything his family stood for.

He always prided himself on his Amish community and how they cared for each other. Going outside the limits of their *g'may* for such matters would go against the *Ordnung*. His family would be called in front of the church if they found out. He didn't think his mother could handle such a scandal. As he tucked the document back into its brown folder, a slip of paper fell to the floor. On it were the names of four of their neighbors, one of which was Bishop Weaver. After each name was a dollar amount, which he assumed was a monthly payment amount. Turning back to the loan agreement, he took notice of the balloon payment due on December 31st. Just a couple of months away.

Instead of returning the folder to its hiding place, he tucked it in his jacket and headed to the stables. It was time to visit Bishop Weaver.

Voices in the storage barn lured Reuben away from the stables. Almer's voice rose above the rest. "It doesn't make sense. Someone had to loosen these bolts. A wheel just doesn't fall off like this."

Almer took his hat off and slapped it against his thigh as he nodded a greeting toward Reuben.

"What's the problem?"

"I think someone tampered with the apple wagon wheel. Someone is messing with us. Just last month, someone put rats in the cold storage." Reuben took notice of his oldest *bruder's* rising wrath. "I tell you; someone is up to no good."

Reuben sent Almer a concerned glance and motioned him outside. "I think we have bigger problems than a broken wagon wheel. Look at this."

Almer opened the folder and shook his head, letting out a low growl. "What has he gotten us into? A loan? We'll never be able to make that payment!"

"Did you know the farm was struggling financially?"

"*Nee,* not until he told us just a few weeks ago."

Reuben handed him the slip of paper. "That's not all. Look at this. Seems like we're not the only ones in a mess."

With an eruption of angry words, Reuben stayed until his *bruder* had calmed down before shedding more light on the dire situation. "*Mamm* showed me this a few minutes ago."

Almer read the note out loud. "*This is your last chance. Meet me at noon at the covered bridge. Life as you know it is at stake. Don't take this warning lightly and bring the box...I know you have it.*"

Almer lifted his hands up in disgust. "What's that supposed to mean? What else has he gotten himself into?" He started to pace back and forth. "I knew it. Someone is trying to sabotage Raber Farms for whatever is in that box." He grabbed the folder back and stuffed both notes back inside. "Come on. It's time we pay a visit to Bishop Weaver."

***

Weaver closed his shop door and slipped the lock to prevent unwanted visitors. As far as their wives knew, the four men were gathering to discuss changes to the *Ordnung* that would be brought up at their next church meeting.

However, the purpose of covering the meaning of their assembly was beyond the truth. All men in attendance had fallen to the same fate as Daniel Raber. Their farms and businesses were held hostage to both Mercer Lending and the group of individuals who strong-armed for Jonathan Mercer.

After quieting the sudden rush of harsh concerns, one of Mose's neighbors spoke up. "I knew he couldn't be trusted. Mercer has had it out for all of us when we wouldn't concede to selling off our farmland. We should have been suspicious when he offered us that short-term loan when the economy tanked last year. Now look at us. We're all as bad off as Daniel."

Another man spoke up. "If we don't find the evidence Daniel gathered, we'll lose everything soon."

Over the last few years, Mose watched and listened carefully to the people in his flock. Some were driven by fear, and some by money. He couldn't help but be dismayed at how he failed to lead them in the ways of the Lord. Many shared the same biblical principles and never veered off the path except when all of them fell to the promises of Mercer Lending, including himself. He was beside himself that he allowed such things to happen.

Small-time farming was becoming increasingly less profitable for their Amish community. And while many of the men held true to tradition, they fell prey to Jonathan's fast cash promises. In his notebook, Mose took careful notes of all payments and went to each farm to collect what was due. Each put their farms and businesses up for collateral and had as much to lose. Daniel went above and beyond trying to find a way out of their loan shark predicament.

Mose hushed the men. "I took the liberty of checking through Daniel's *haus* and found nothing. I'll discuss it with him when he's up for visitors. The last time we spoke, he was waiting for one more piece of information before we could confront Mercer. Until then, we'll need to make our payment on time and in full."

Someone asked, "Did you check the office?

"I'm sure he wouldn't keep it where Saloma could find it."

"*Nee*...the door was locked, and I didn't want to break in. He'll tell me where it is as soon as he's able."

Mose was tired and too old to struggle to hold it together like he was. In all his years as the bishop, he never dreamed he would have fallen to such sin. It was one thing to take out a loan to save his business; it was another to lie about it. If the other ministers and members of his *g'may* found out what they did, he'd be dismissed. The shame of it all was too much to bear. How could he face the community when they found out he failed them in such an unrespectable manner? He had to find Daniel's evidence quickly.

A sudden thunderous knock on the shop door pulled Mose's attention away. All the men shuddered when Almer and Reuben stood outside as Mose opened the door.

Without even so much as a greeting, Almer handed Bishop Weaver the folder and said, "I think we have a problem, and we're certain you have the answers we're looking for."

Mose looked over their shoulders before closing the door. "It's trouble for sure and one we're unsure how to get out of."

Almer seethed. "I'd say it's more than trouble. We're all about to lose everything we've worked hard to build. How could you all be so stupid as to sign such a thing?"

Mose mumbled, "It was a bait and switch scheme, and we didn't realize it until we were so deep in debt, we couldn't get out." Mose wiped his brow before continuing. "But your father was collecting proof, and we almost had enough to set Curtman straight."

Reuben asked, "Curtman from Curtman's Apple Orchard?"

"*Jah*. We found out he's behind Mercer Lending. They've been threatening all of us. And strange things have been happening on each of our farms."

"Like messing with the bolts on our wagon?" Reuben asked.

Bishop Weaver sighed. "We're certain of it. Daniel was getting close and asking too many questions, and we're certain Curtman and Mercer got word."

Mose groaned. "We've got to find that box. Your father has it hidden somewhere; we just don't know where."

CHAPTER 12

Allie turned off the diesel generator to the wringer washer and balanced the clothes basket on her hip as she exited the basement. Already tired from her Monday morning chores, she used the basket's weight to open the screen door leading to the side porch. The squeaky hinge echoed as it slammed behind her, scattering a small flock of barn swallows hovering at the bird feeder.

It had been almost a month since they returned to Willow Springs, and the ongoing tension between Saloma and Reuben intensified whenever she was around. She kept the strain she caused at bay by throwing herself into learning how to be a good Amish *fraa*. Out to prove to her new mother-in-law that she could adapt to simpler Amish ways, she fought hard to fit in.

197

Her father-in-law was a source of concern as his recovery took a toll on Reuben and his *bruders*.

Even though a cool mist hung in the air, beads of sweat formed on her upper lip as her mouth watered and she swallowed hard, trying to keep from being sick.

Rounding the corner of the house, a flutter of blue and black in Lydia's yard caught her eye. If it weren't for the older woman's friendship, Allie might have packed it in and returned to Sugarcreek without looking back.

"Not again," she whispered under her breath. "How did she get her laundry out so early?"

Dropping the basket to the ground, she sighed as she bent down and picked up a pair of Rueben's pants. She snapped them hard to release the wrinkles and pinned them to the line. The morning sun was starting to rise above the clothesline as she peered into Lydia's yard. She hoped the woman wasn't outside and wouldn't notice how late she was in getting her laundry hung out to dry.

Noticing the haphazard way she hung her clothes, Allie remembered how her mom's clothesline always looked like a kaleidoscope of colors. She rustled in the basket, sorting the colors to hang them in neat blue, black, and white rows. If her life felt like a mangled mess, the least she could do was hang her laundry orderly.

A wave of homesickness overcame her as she looked at the place she now called home. No matter how hard she tried, she felt like she was failing at being a good *fraa* to Reuben.

It took all her effort to get the laundry washed and out of the line. Just that morning, she woke up to the lingering smell of burnt meatloaf, which instantly made her sick to her stomach. She couldn't even pull herself out of bed to make Reuben's lunch, which certainly didn't help with her current mood.

As she pinned the last towel to the line and pushed the basket closer to the pole, Allie turned her face toward the sky and said a silent prayer.

Lord, please help me be a good wife to Reuben. Help me find joy in my home today, and most of all, help me not to burn dinner tonight.

At the table, sipping peppermint tea to soothe her stomach, she started making a list of all she needed to accomplish. Above everything else, she wanted to make Reuben his favorite gingersnap cookies. A lump formed in her throat as she thought about sending him off without breakfast or lunch. What was her problem? Why was she so tired that she couldn't even force herself to get up with him that morning?

Enough is enough, she thought to herself. *There's no sense in feeling sorry for myself. I'm not going to get this list done by just looking at it.* Forcing herself up, she put her cup in the sink. Out the window, she saw Lydia working in her garden.

"There she is again. Doesn't she ever stop?" Allie spoke out loud this time, even though no one could hear her.

Looking across the road, she saw the short, round woman bent over, pulling the last of the winter squash. She reached up and rubbed the back of her neck as she closed her eyes and blew out a long breath. Without thinking again, she grabbed her sweater off the peg by the front door and staggered outside. She wasn't going to be outdone by a seventy-year-old woman.

Before heading out the door, a wave of nausea stopped her, and she leaned over the kitchen sink. Splashing cold water on her face, she thought. *A little upset stomach isn't going to stop me.* When she sauntered around the house, Lydia had moved from the garden and was kneeling in a flower bed.

Tucking a few loose strands of hair back under her covering, a wave of loneliness gave her enough nerve to approach her friend. Why did she feel the need to keep up with her? What made her feel so inferior that she pushed herself to outdo the older woman? *Stop this,* she thought. *Just go talk to her.*

At the spot where Lydia was working, Allie just stood and stared. Lydia's gray hair was coming loose from the bun secured at the back of her neck, and the wind blew her blue scarf over her head. She started the conversation by taking a cleansing breath and willing herself to speak.

"How do you do it?"

Startled, Lydia looked over her shoulder, only to see Allie, arms crossed over her chest, standing at the sidewalk's edge.

"My goodness, dear, you scared me. You shouldn't sneak up on an old woman like that."

"I'm sorry. I didn't mean to scare you."

"What's the problem, child? You look like you're about to cry."

"I feel like such a failure and need to talk to someone."

Lydia stood and walked over to her. Putting her arm around Allie's shoulders, she guided her to the porch.

"Come, let's go sit, and you can tell me what's bothering you."

Before they even got to the porch, a sob caught in the back of her throat, and she made a funny hiccup sound as she reached into her apron pocket for a hankie. Giving her a chance to calm down, Lydia paused. "I just made a fresh batch of sugar cookies this morning," she said. "How about I make us tea and bring a few? Then we can talk."

"Do you need some help?"

"*Nee*, you just sit here; I'll be right back."

Making herself comfortable in one of the willow rockers that flanked Lydia's front door, Allie looked across the road at her new home. Just yesterday, she painted a fresh coat of blue paint on the front door, reminding her that her painting was why she burned the meatloaf. The new pleated curtains she made last week looked beautiful against the windows she had worked so hard at to get years' worth of dirt and grime off of.

Why was she having such a hard time appreciating all that *Gott* had provided her? Not once had Ruben complained about the meatloaf. He even went as far as having a second piece, even when she knew it was barely edible.

Pushing the screen door open with her foot, Lydia carried a wooden tray and set it on the stand beside her chair.

"*Ya* know we moved to Willow Springs from Lancaster when I was just about your age." Lydia paused for a moment. "If I remember correctly, I'd just gotten married myself." She giggled as she settled back in her chair to get comfortable.

"Boy, did I mess things up when I first got married. I thought everything had to be perfect. Being the new girl in town, I felt everyone was watching everything I did. I thought the house needed to be cleaned until it shined, fresh bread made every day, the laundry on the line by eight o'clock every Monday morning, not a weed in the garden, and not a hair out of place. I was running myself ragged trying to keep everything just so. I was so obsessed with keeping the *haus* and proving to everyone I had it all together that I forgot the most important thing."

Allie leaned in, hoping to learn Lydia's secret. "What was it? What's the most important thing?"

Lydia leaned in and whispered, "I was trying to please the wrong person."

Sitting back in her chair, she continued. "I was prideful, and I was comparing myself to others instead of trying to please the one that means the most. It was my husband who brought it to my attention. And even though I didn't like to hear it, he reminded me that my primary focus was to please *Gott* and that I was to humbly serve Him with all my heart in all areas of my life, including keeping house. Once I realized I didn't need to prove anything to anyone else, I fell into my natural rhythm of being a good *fraa*."

Taking a sip of her tea and setting it back down, Allie hoped it would calm her queasiness as she listened intently to Lydia's story.

"Keeping a home is more than having a spotless house. It's about serving *Gott* with a happy heart, no matter where we are in life," Lydia said soothingly. "When we do that, it can't help but spill over to being a good and faithful *fraa* to our *mun*. Now, tell me, why are you feeling like a failure?"

"Oh, Lydia, you have no idea how I needed to hear those words today. I've been beating myself up for weeks, and you're so right; I've been killing myself trying to prove to Reuben's mother I'm worthy of their family. But most of all, I haven't once thought about being a *fraa* having anything to do with serving *Gott*. I've made such a mess of things. I've been grumpy with Reuben and feeling sorry for myself since we moved here. Poor Reuben can't do anything right, and he's gone out of his way trying to make things easier for me. He knows I'm struggling with his mother, but I'm trying not to make matters worse."

Stopping to blow her nose, Allie stuffed the used tissue in her sleeve and reached for her tea again. Holding the cup to her mouth, she gently blew on the hot liquid, taking time to gather her thoughts.

"I'm embarrassed to tell you I couldn't even pull myself out of bed this morning to make Reuben's breakfast, and I sent him to work without any lunch. I'm so tired all the time, and I'm crying over everything so much I'm making myself sick every morning. Do you remember feeling this way when you got married?"

"Oh child, do I ever, and I felt that way seven times."

"Seven times! Oh no, I won't put myself or Reuben through this seven times."

Allie watched as Lydia tried hiding her mouth with her hand, and a small giggle escaped. "I don't think you're going to have much control over that," she said, shaking her head. "If *Gott* says you'll go through it seven times, then you'll go through it seven times."

"No, I won't; I'm done with feeling like this," Allie replied, trying to sound brave despite the quaver in her voice. "Thank you so much. I feel better now. I just needed to talk things out, and you gave me a lot to think about. I'd better head home. I want to make Reuben his favorite dessert. Maybe he'll forgive me for not getting up with him this morning."

Standing up and placing her cup on the tray, Allie skipped down the steps with a new sense of purpose.

"Thanks for the tea and cookies," she hollered. "I'll have to get that recipe. I think Reuben would like them."

Still seated, Lydia pushed the rocker in motion. She waited until Allie almost made it to the road before she hollered, "He'll forgive you as soon as you tell him."

Allie stopped in her tracks.

"Tell him what?"

"You're with child."

"I'm what?"

Allie returned to the porch and looked confused at Lydia's strange comment.

"A baby, you silly girl."

Lydia's comment caught her off guard, and she just stared at her as she let her words sink in.

"Could it be? I've been so busy trying to get everything just so with the house I never gave being pregnant a second thought?"

Lydia walked down the steps, put her arm around her shoulders, and pulled her closer. "I think you're confused about what you're experiencing with morning sickness. I'm no midwife, but I'd go home and look at your monthly calendar. I can bet *Gott* has His own plans for little Miss Allie, which might include why you've been feeling so out of sorts."

Allie leaned her head on her older friend's shoulder. "How could I have been so consumed with my pity party that I didn't see the obvious? I have so much to explain to Reuben. Both about the baby and the whole part about being a servant to the Lord in every area of our lives. You've taught me so much. And just think, when I came here today, I was mad that you always seemed to have everything together, and I couldn't keep up with you."

Lydia squeezed Allie's forearm. "First of all, we don't give our *muns* enough credit, and I bet he already has an inkling about your problem. He may very well be waiting for you to figure it out yourself. It could be why he let you stay in bed this morning and didn't say a word about sending him to work without lunch. And second, I still need to have everything together and organized. I learned a long time ago to find my joy in the Lord. I can't find it in a clean house or in-laws. Nor in people, and I certainly can't find it in myself without the help of *Gott*."

Patting Allie's hand, Lydia gave her a gentle push. "Now, how about you go home and make Reuben cookies and then take a walk to the phone shanty and make an appointment with the midwife in town? I may not be your *mamm*, but I can lend an ear if you need to talk. My door is always open."

Allie felt tears spring to her eyes.

"Oh, Lydia, thank you so much," she said, words spilling in gratitude. "How did I get so lucky to have you as a neighbor and friend? I can't wait to write to my family and tell them about your kindness."

Waving over her shoulder and walking with a lighter step, Allie was excited for Reuben to get home. Between Lydia's motherly advice and putting all the pieces together about why she'd been so tired, it looked like *Gott* already had planned how this day would turn out.

Lydia was right, Allie realized. It was time she started to find joy in the Lord and serve Him with the heart of a humble servant. At that instant, she realized she had so much to be thankful for, and none of it revolved around how clean her house was or what her mother-in-law thought of her. What mattered most was right in front of her; it took her new friend to point it out to her.

Stopping at the mailbox before returning to the house, Allie fell to the steps when she opened the letter with no return address. Gasping and holding her hand to her throat, she moaned. "She's gone too far."

Allie had moved her hand from her mouth and rubbed small circles across her tummy, mumbling, "How dare she? How on earth does she think she has any right to threaten such things?"

She reread the words...

Don't get too comfortable in Willow Springs. Your marriage will be annulled if it's the last thing I do.

The letter wasn't signed, but there was no doubt in Allie's mind where or who it came from.

She patted her belly and whispered, "You're too late to do anything about it."

Allie felt her face warm and thought. *Can she really do this? If Saloma believes for one minute I'm going to sit back and let her get away with this, she has another think coming.*

A rush of annoyance surfaced as she tried to calm herself down. *Don't get all worked up. Wait until Reuben gets home. He'll know how to handle his mother. On second thought, perhaps I need to handle things on my own. The last thing Reuben needs is to play referee between the two of us. Enough is enough.*

CHAPTER 13

A blind sense of obligation hung over Reuben as he descended the long lane leading to Raber Farms. Concern for both Allie and his father weighed heavy on his brow. Allie was undoubtedly suffering from the effects of his mother's hurtful welcome, so much so he was at a loss as to how to handle their current situation.

While he was relieved his father stepped in about letting them stay in the *doddi haus*, he couldn't deny his mother was making life a challenge. Slipping out before Allie awoke, he prayed she wouldn't be upset that he didn't wake her. It was becoming increasingly difficult to see the look of weariness in her eyes. A low grumble in his stomach intensified as the aroma of bacon wafted in the air, forcing him to follow it toward the kitchen.

He stopped momentarily to scratch Bishop Weaver's horse's nose when mumbled voices made their way around the porch, stopping on the other side of the buggy. Unaware of his presence, he stayed hidden and listened to his mother's sharp words.

"I want you to take care of this issue and quickly. I want her out of here."

With mock seriousness, the bishop answered, "How often do I have to tell you it's not my concern?"

His mother's reply came like vinegar, making him ill just listening. *What had happened to sour her like this?* He thought. A sense of embarrassment hovered over him at the spectacle she was making by involving the bishop in a private family matter. *Datt would be furious,* he thought. But still, he stopped and eavesdropped on their conversation.

"Gold digger, for sure. I'm certain she's dug her claws into Reuben for his money and status in the community."

The old man snorted a laugh. "You can't be serious."

"I am, and I want you to find a reason to annul their marriage."

"I can't do that. Especially if they didn't get married in an Amish church."

"Exactly! They didn't get married in the eyes of the church. They went about everything half backward."

With severe authority, he stated, "In all my days of being the bishop of this community, I've never had such an outlandish request." An awkward silence fell, and he boldly stated, "Denied."

The words from his mother's mouth mortified Reuben, and he couldn't believe anyone could be so hurtful. Any luck he could reason with her about her bizarre behavior was lost instantly as she snarled, "You seem to forget what I know about Catherine and your *schwester*. Wouldn't the church like to know why your *schwester* ran away?"

Reuben didn't need to see Weaver's face to know his mother crossed the line. His following words, more of a subtle command, replied, "It's about time we take this up with Daniel."

Their voices faded as his mother trotted after him as they returned to the kitchen. Her taxing plea to keep things to themselves fell on deaf ears even after the back door slammed.

A hollow spot lodged in Reuben's throat as he tried to comprehend what his mother could be referring to. But more importantly, how she could go to such lengths to get rid of Allie.

He walked away, hanging his head while thinking. *It was a mistake bringing Allie back here.* And he declared. *As soon as Datt gets on his feet, we're moving to Sugarcreek.*

Almer nodded toward the bishop's buggy as Reuben made his way to the side of the cider press. "What's he doing here?"

Still mulling over what he heard, he mumbled, "Business with *Mamm*, I assume."

"Perhaps he's come to ask *Datt* about the infamous box?"

Reuben leaned on the door and asked, "What do you think ever happened to *Mamm* to make her like she is?"

"Who knows? But my *fraa* thinks it's a heart issue."

"How so?"

"Not sure…maybe she's holding onto something that's been festering all these years."

"But why take it out on Allie?"

Almer laughed. "It's just her turn."

In one swift moment, he remembered every sordid detail. His mother put each of his *bruder's* wives through the same torment. Absurd accusations and belligerent conversations to the point that each woman bowed down or stayed away. "Is that why they don't come around much?"

Taking turns dumping crates of apples on the conveyor, they sorted through the bins of ugly apples, removing any spoiled ones before sending them off to the washing station. "They come around to help bottle cider, but I can guarantee it's not high on their list." Almer sneered. "My Annie will find any excuse in the books not to help."

"I guess not working on the farm daily, I didn't get to see how bad it really was." Reuben struggled to see it from the other side and continued to sift through the apples before asking, "Why do you think *datt* allows it?"

He expected his *bruder* to answer, hoping he would have an explanation. When the silence turned into a few minutes, Reuben added, "Maybe it's easier to lay a blind eye, *jah*?"

Almer dumped another bin on the belt. "She's not always been like this. Seems to have gotten worse as each of us has left home." Wiping his hands on the rag tucked behind his suspender, Almer continued. "Annie says the devil has ahold of *Mamm's* tongue."

Reuben thought glumly of the conversation he'd overheard and wondered if there was any truth to Annie's observation. Refusing to breathe life into such things, he replied, "I highly doubt that's the case."

"I call it as I see it." Almer snorted.

Bishop Weaver stood in the doorway and yelled over the diesel engine driving the conveyor belt to get their attention.

After Almer shut it off, he asked, "Any luck asking *datt* about the box?"

"*Nee*, we had other things to discuss, and he was in no mood to entertain me further after our brief conversation."

His tone turned serious. "Reuben, may I have a word with you?"

Lifting an eyebrow in Almer's direction, Reuben followed the older gentleman outside. Without an ounce of pleasantries, the bishop asked, "Your *mamm* has some concerns about your recent marriage. Any reason I should be concerned as well?"

With a vague sense of unease, Reuben stated, "I don't take marriage lightly."

"As you shouldn't in the eyes of the Lord."

Reuben fought to keep his voice steady. "I had no other choice than to marry Allie in Florida."

"How old is she?"

"Eighteen."

"With child?"

The implied accusation set Reuben's jaw to twitch before he responded. "*Nee.*"

The bishop glanced sharply at him. "Then why the hurry?"

Reuben added, while trying to maintain a level of composure at the bishop's intrusive questioning. "It's just what I felt I wanted to do."

For a moment, Reuben noticed a glimmer of sympathy on the old man's face as he processed his answer. Without another word about his decision, the bishoped asked, "Will you be joining the church?"

The dreaded question and the one sure to set his mother in a new tailspin, he retorted, "*Jah.* But not the Old Order. I think Allie will be more comfortable in the New Order Fellowship."

In a shocking act of acceptance, the bishop shook Reuben's hand. "As a bishop, I've walked many families through great and complicated conflicts." He hesitated momentarily, leaving Reuben to wonder where he was going with his statement. "Healing begins when forgiveness is offered."

Noticing the sudden tightness around the bishop's mouth, Reuben wondered if the old man was talking about his forgiveness or something he and Allie had to work through with his mother. Before departing, the bishop returned to where Almer was working, and Reuben followed.

"It's almost the end of the month, and a payment is due on our loan. Will you boys be able to come up with your share?"

Almer frowned in annoyance. "I doubt we have a choice, *jah*?"

Bishop Weaver fingered his jaw thoughtfully. "I'd hoped we could have cleared this up by now. But without your *datt's* evidence, we have no choice but to make another payment."

Almer dried his hands. "What exactly are you hoping this so-called evidence will prove?"

"That Curtman's business dealings are not on the up and up and that we have proof that he and Mercer have unethically changed the loan terms."

Reuben stiffened. "Even if we have proof, you all signed a legal document. It certainly isn't going to get us out of paying off the loan."

"*Nee*, it won't, and we have no plan not to pay what is due, but it will forgo the balloon payment and the risk of our farms and businesses going into foreclosure."

Almer grunted, "You really think a few threats from us will make a difference? We aren't in the business of forceful tactics."

The stout man's nod was brief. "Just because we're pacifists doesn't mean we can't be smart. Force isn't the only way to deliver justice."

Reuben nodded his head slyly. "What makes you think whatever *datt* came up with will make a difference?"

"Because Curtman has been buying up land all over the tri-state area, trying to monopolize the produce industry. His goal is to put small-time farms like ours out of business, and he's not shy about using shady methods."

Almer added fresh tobacco to his pipe and asked, "And Mercer Lending, what do they have to do with all of this?"

"This is the proof your father was gathering. Seems like Mercer has spent some time in jail for racketeering. The authorities get word of his bait and switch scheme, and he'll land himself back in jail."

Almer puffed intently, losing himself in the tobacco, before responding. "So that's the leverage you want to use to cancel the balloon payment?"

"Exactly. That's why it's so important we talk to your *datt* and find that box."

Almer nodded, puffed out smoke, and turned toward the door. "No time like the present."

***

Saloma sat on the edge of the bed, trembling on the verge of panic as she recalled the intimidating way Mose spoke to both her and Daniel. His tone was sharp and threatening as he warned her to stop dredging up the past for her own gain.

The look on Daniel's face when Mose told him what she had asked him to do was agonizing. All it did was add another level of pain to Daniel's recovery. After the bishop had left, Daniel didn't say a word but sent her away with a flip of his hand. Often, his silence was worse than any confrontation and twice as discomforting.

Throwing herself into household chores, she had carried a scrub brush and bucket to the bedroom, hoping to chase the agony away with hard work. Lowering to her knees, she got busy scrubbing the hardwood floors. Clenching the wooden brush, she made continuous circles while conversing with herself.

No one understands the depth of loneliness a mother feels when her children all leave. Why can't anyone see Reuben is making a terrible decision by bringing an outsider into our lives? She'll pull him away from me for sure and certain.

She moaned and wiped her forehead before pushing the bed out of the way.

Mose, out of everyone, should see that. Letting someone from the outside in only causes strife and family division. Look what they had to do to protect their family name because of allowing someone into their tight-knit community.

Sliding the bucket across the floor, it stopped and splashed water out as it hit a raised board.

Using the towel she'd slung over her shoulder to mop up the spill, she pressed on the loose board, releasing it from the rest of the floor. Inside was a small tin box. "What on earth?" she mumbled as she retrieved it from its hiding spot. Sitting back on her heels, she took a few minutes to sift through its contents. Confused as to what most of it meant, she was sure it was the box the note had alluded to and knew she had to discuss it with

Daniel. Returning the box to its hiding place, she moved the bed back and finished with the floor.

No sooner had she dumped the bucket of water down the sink than Allie showed up at her back door uninvited. When Saloma answered the door, the two women glared at one another through the screen until Allie spoke up. "You might as well let me in because I'm not going anywhere until we discuss this." Allie held up the letter.

"I have nothing more to say. I made it perfectly clear."

Allie pulled the screen door open and pushed her way inside. "All you did is add more strife to our relationship. Can't you see what having us at odds for no good reason is doing to Reuben?"

Saloma crossed her arms and stood firmly. "I don't have time for this today. And besides, I don't throw out idle threats. I will find a way to void this marriage; you can count on that."

"On what grounds?"

"That Reuben wasn't in his sound mind, and you tricked him."

With a quick gesture of disgust, Allie laughed. "Tricked him? And how do you think I did that?"

Saloma scoffed. "I know how you girls work. You see a wealthy family, and you dig your heels in deep."

Allie raised her voice. "You think I went after Reuben's money? The last time I checked, I don't think he's getting a stipend from Raber Farms."

Saloma let out a short snort. "Just get out of here. I said I don't have time for this."

Allie moved closer. "I'm not leaving until you tell me what I did to you that makes you despise me."

"I don't have to explain myself to you."

"Yes, *yes*, you do." Allie sucked in her breath and squared her shoulders. "Whether you like it or not, we're married, and you can't do anything about it."

Saloma's speech thickened. "We'll see about that."

Allie laid her hand across her stomach and grinned. "No...you see, you're too late."

Saloma's face turned pale, and she tripped, reaching for a chair and sinking to the floor. When Allie tried to help, Saloma snapped her arm away and moved a hand to her temple. "Get out I said. I want you out of my *haus*!"

Allie waited until her mother-in-law could pull herself back into the chair. When Saloma's ill attempts to right herself failed,

Allie moved in again to help. "Quit fighting me. Let me at least help you up."

Her voice, now a little unsteady, slurred unpleasantries as Allie helped her up. After seeing her upright, she handed her a glass of water just as a bell rang from the other room. It took Saloma a few minutes to register the noise, and it alarmed Allie as she seemed to be squinting or trying to focus unsuccessfully. The bell rang again, and Saloma pointed to the front room.

Allie followed the sound into the bedroom off the living room. Her father-in-law met her with a questioning stare. "Are you the reason for all the commotion out there?"

"*Jah*, I upset her. Sorry about that."

His eyes softened. "She's easily distressed these days." Daniel struggled to pull himself up in a more comfortable position, and Allie was quick to help him adjust the pillows.

"She said she was going to bring me something to drink. That was fifteen minutes ago. Is she doing that now?"

Allie looked over her shoulder and stuttered. "Uhm…no, I don't think so. She tripped, and I had to help her up."

"Again? She's been doing a lot of that lately. Is she okay?"

"I'll go check, and then I'll bring you back a glass of meadow tea. Is that good?"

"*Jah.*" A hearty, contagious smile met her. "Allie?"

"Yes?"

"Don't be too hard on her. She means well."

Allie gave him a long, level look. "I'm not sure what I've done to upset her."

"Believe me, it's not you. She has difficulty letting go of her boys and fights hard to keep them nearby. Most of the time to her own fault."

"But she hasn't even given me a chance."

He cast her an approving look. "You'll do fine. You're exactly what this family needs, and she'll come around once she realizes it."

With a quick intake of breath, she said, "I sure hope you're right."

He pointed to the newspaper and waited for her to hand it before adding, "I know you've not done what she's accusing you of."

Allie felt at ease with her new father-in-law and sent a silent prayer of thankfulness for his kindness. Words escaped her as she turned and left, a hopeful smile on her face.

As soon as she made her way back into the kitchen, she watched as Saloma slithered from her chair back to the floor. A panicked look settled in Saloma's eyes, and her breathing became fast and labored. Kneeling beside her, Allie took her hand. "What is it? Are you okay?"

With wide eyes and raised eyebrows, Saloma tried to form words, but nothing came. She grasped Allie's hand and started to shake.

Before she could holler for help, Reuben and Almer walked in the back door. "Go quickly," she yelled. "I think she's having a stroke. We need an ambulance."

Almer ran back out the door, and Reuben knelt beside them. "*Mamm,* where does it hurt?"

With a dazed and confused look, Saloma stared at them without answering. "Try to lift your arms. Can you do that, *Mamm?*" Reuben demanded.

Allie whispered, "I don't think she can. Look at her mouth; the corner is drooping. Reuben, I really think she's had a stroke."

Reuben took off his jacket and put it under her head. "Hang on, *Mamm,* Almer went to get help."

Allie backed away and observed Reuben's tenderness. Regardless of how she'd been acting, she was still his mother, and Allie could tell he loved her.

From the other room, her father-in-law bellowed, "What's going on out there?"

Reuben looked up at Allie with unsure eyes. "Don't worry, I'll take care of *datt*; you keep her comfortable until the ambulance gets here, and don't let her fall asleep. Keep talking to her."

A tingly shiver ran up Allie's arm as she followed her father-in-law's voice to the bedroom. A dark cloud seemed to form over the Raber *haus* as Allie explained to Daniel that tragedy had struck their lives again.

CHAPTER 14

Allie cut a fresh slice of cake and handed it to her father-in-law. "Here, taste this." She held her breath as he took a big bite and only exhaled after he smiled and nodded his head. "It would be a tasty addition to the sweets we could offer in the Apple Barn next year, *jah*?"

"It's quite tasty, I'll give you that. If I don't get on my feet, the boys will soon have to roll me out to the barn with all the taste testing I'm doing for you."

Allie hadn't always been good at baking. But over the last month or so, when she had so much time, she fell in love with trying new recipes. Using Saloma's huge farmhouse kitchen had been so much more enjoyable. She had the best of everything an Amish woman could want.

With Saloma recovering from her stroke at the local rehabilitation center and Daniel unable to care for himself, Allie and Reuben moved into the big farmhouse.

Allie opened the notebook she'd been adding to and wrote down her latest creation. For the last week, she and Daniel started to come up with some ideas on how they could revitalize Raber Farms.

Allie tapped her pencil on the table. "So, do you like the brown butter frosting, or would it be better with cream cheese icing? Could you tell I sweetened it with raw honey from your bee hives?"

Daniel gave her a wide-tooth grin. "I think it's perfect just the way it is." He paused long enough to sip his coffee before asking, "All these sweet treats sound wonderful, but who's going to have time to do all this baking?" He smiled again and nodded his head toward her middle. "You'll have your hands full with a little one this time next year."

She balanced her chin in the palm of her hand as she leaned on the table, giving serious thought to his question. "I've actually been pondering that. I was thinking about asking Emma and Katie from Yoder's Bakery if they would be willing to provide the baked goods we would need to keep the store stocked. I could give them my recipes, and we just pay them a portion."

Adding another note to the paper in front of her, she continued. "I know we won't make as much profit on those items, but I don't want to take business away from their bakery by adding one in the Apple Barn. That wouldn't be good for the community." Waiting to see how he felt about her ideas, she sipped tea.

Daniel picked up a pencil and pulled the notebook over. "We'd need to run the numbers. If we take the percentage Yoder's charge and then add our markup, we can figure out our rate of return on each product. That should tell us if adding baked goods to our inventory is profitable. "

Her tongue flicked out and wetted her lips, which produced a lingering smile. Clapping her hands, she exclaimed, "This is so exciting. Do you think the boys will go for our idea of making Raber Farms a fall and winter attraction instead of just a produce farm?"

He gave her an amused smile and let her rattle on.

"It could be a true destination spot for Northwestern Pennsylvania. We could do hayrides and sell pumpkins. Even make cider donuts." She stopped long enough to lean her chin in her hand. "I can see it now. People from all over the county would travel here for family outings."

Daniel folded his fingers together and dropped them below his chin. "Lots of changes would need to take place. But I'm starting to see your vision."

Allie's voice trailed on. "And then Christmas. Do you think the bishop would allow us to sell Christmas trees? We could do sleigh rides and sell hot chocolate."

"Whoa, now. Let's concentrate on one season at a time."

"*Nee*, but we can't. If we're going to sell trees, we'll need to start planting them right away. It will take years to get them big enough to sell. The *Englisch* love forging through the fields looking for the perfect tree."

Daniel was quick to point out. "You know we live in an Amish community where Christmas trees and such are looked down upon. All these things that appeal to the *Englisch*? I'm not sure our Amish neighbors will enjoy all the attention."

Her words flowed swiftly and efficiently. "I've already thought about that. So many Amish cottage businesses in Willow Springs could display their products in the store. Many Amish merchants rely on tourist sales in the summer, giving them another place to increase sales."

Daniel smiled at her amusing argument. "I have to agree that's one way to sell the bishop on it. If we're helping our community survive this downturn in farming, he may just approve it."

Allie smiled and eagerly wrote her ideas down on paper and added, "And you've not heard the best yet."

"Oh...no. I'm afraid to ask what else you have up your sleeve."

Her smile widened as she leaned in, ready to share a life-changing secret. "I think the storage barn would make the perfect venue for weddings."

Daniel cocked an eyebrow her way. "I think that's going too far for even me to approve of."

"Now hear me out," she begged. "We could have a catering kitchen that both the Amish and *Englisch* could utilize. There is plenty of room to host more than three hundred people, and with all the ample parking space and the horse corral for the Amish, it's the perfect solution. I tell you, there is no place like it in all of Lawrence County."

Daniel sat back and rested his elbows on the chair arms. "The *Englisch* would require power, not sure that would pass by the bishop."

"But why not? He allows power at Shetler's Grocery to run the refrigeration. What differentiates us from other businesses catering to Amish and *Englisch*?" Allie held her cup in both hands and near her lips before continuing. "Weddings could be a way to generate income in the spring and summer months. That way, we'll have a constant influx of money throughout the year."

Allie waited for him to contemplate what she was proposing and watched his face turn serious. "You've given me a lot to ponder, and I promise I'll take each of your ideas and give them a lot of thought. But you know I can't do anything until I talk to the boys and discuss things with Saloma."

Allie nodded approvingly even though inside she felt a twinge of anxiety with the notion that it would take Saloma's approval for any of her projects to come to life.

Muffled voices drew her attention away as Almer and Reuben walked in the back door. After hanging his black felt hat and jacket on the peg by the backdoor, Reuben laid his hand on Allie's shoulder for a moment before sitting beside her.

"How's your *mamm* today?" she asked tenderly.

With a tense posture, Reuben replied, "We met with her doctor today, and her progress is slow. They indicated that they have done as much as possible and suggested we bring her home."

Allie tried to hide her apprehension. "They feel we're capable of caring for her needs here?"

Almer nodded with a tentative smile. "Her speech is still affected from the stroke, but they've been able to get her to walk with a cane a short distance." Almer moved to the stove to pour a cup of coffee. "She has limited control of her right arm, but they taught her to compensate with her left."

An awkward silence fell as they all struggled to find a way to care for both her and Daniel. It was Almer who broke the quiet with the inevitable. "*Datt*, we're not sure what to do. I've talked to the boys, and our *fraas* are busy caring for the *kinner*. And you know *Mamm*, she's not made it easy on any of them to be willing to go out of their way to help." Almer looked warmly at Allie. "And that includes her."

Allie felt her insides tumble, wishing she could talk to Reuben privately. She wasn't sure she could handle his mother alone and care for his *datt* all at once. Daniel was easy, and they had bonded by spending so much time together. But Saloma, that was a different story. She studied Reuben's face, hoping to discover his feelings.

After another wary pause, Daniel rubbed his elevated leg and asked, "When do they want to release her?"

Reuben was quick to point out, "The day after tomorrow." He hesitated, gauging his words before continuing. "They also gave us the name of an assisted living facility we could send her to if we didn't have anyone to care for her properly."

Allie watched her father-in-law as he responded with an absent stare. It wasn't hard for her to comprehend what was going on behind his dark and worried eyes. Saloma might be hard to handle and a thorn in most of her family's eyes, but to Daniel, she was the woman he loved.

In no more than a whisper, Allie said, "There's no need to do that. Bring her home."

***

Reuben watched as Allie stared up at the clock on the kitchen wall, willing it to stop. "I'm not looking forward to this." Her voice was soft yet sincere, and her expression was set in a scowl. A tinge of regret at allowing her to agree to take care of his mother floated through his conscience.

"It's not too late to change your mind. I'm sure we can hire a nurse to sit with her."

There was a long pause, then she said, "Your *datt* can't afford that and besides, it's not our way. We are to care for our parents regardless." She paused and then added, "It's what the Lord instructs."

He frowned and felt an extreme surge of guilt. "I..."

"Stop." Allie reached over and took his hand. "There is no other way. I'm the only person in this family who doesn't have other obligations that would keep me from caring for your parents. It's what families do, regardless of how hard it may be."

"But my mother isn't like..."

"I know how your mother is." She pressed her lips together in a tight line.

He couldn't believe how giving she was after his mother treated her so cruelly. "I'll do what I can to help."

Allie stood and kissed his cheek. "You'll do no such thing. You have too much work to do yourself." She carried their breakfast dishes to the counter and added, "I was just bellyaching a little, don't mind me.

I'm over it now. Besides, your *datt* is a joy, and we've had fun the last few weeks getting to know one another. I'm sure he'll act as a buffer as best as he can regarding your *mamm*."

Reuben pulled her down on his lap and rested his hand on her middle. "Promise me you'll do nothing to jeopardize this little one."

She pushed his hand away and stood as Almer entered the back door. "The driver's here. Are you ready?"

Reuben gave Allie one last look, wishing he could remove the line furrowing her brow. She forced a smile at his glance and pushed him to the door. "Really, I'll be fine. Now go. I'm sure the nurses at the care center are anxious for you to pick her up."

After they left, she sank back down in a chair and sipped tea as she watched nuthatches take their breakfast at the suet block she'd hung the day before. Daniel enjoyed sitting at the kitchen window watching the birds as his leg healed. Yesterday, he had her move two rockers from the front room to the kitchen so Saloma could join him.

Just as the clock chimed nine, Lydia knocked on the kitchen door. Allie waved her in. "What a sweet surprise. What has you out and about so early?"

The elderly neighbor grinned in response and handed her a blackberry pie. "Morning does not dawn with the first bird's song."

Allie giggled. "And what's that supposed to mean?"

"Oh, it's just an old German Proverb that means I start my day long before the birds do."

Inhaling the sweet scent, Allie asked, "Is that almond I smell?"

"*Jah*, my secret ingredient. I hope you like it."

"I'll certainly let you know. Feels too hot to cut right now, but if it weren't, I'd be sampling it."

Lydia pulled a chair out, and Allie held up her cup, asking if she'd like some as the older woman got comfortable. "I hear Saloma is coming home today."

Allie whined desperately. "Yes." She leaned back in her chair and added, "I'd be lying if I didn't admit I'm a little apprehensive. She's going to be a handful, to say the least."

"Is she mobile?"

"Reuben says she can walk with a cane even though one leg drags some, and she has some lingering control issues with her right hand. Other than that, her biggest difficulty is speaking. She still isn't talking."

"Might be good for her to listen more than talk right now, and that could be a blessing for you. She can't very well badger you if she can't speak."

A small smile turned up one side of Allie's mouth. "I suppose that's a way to look at it. But still, I'm sure she'll make things difficult for me. I'm the last person in the world she would want to take care of her. And the last we spoke of it, Reuben and Almer hadn't told her we moved in."

Lydia sipped her tea before commenting. "Well, I guess she's in for a big surprise then, isn't she?"

"I'm afraid she'll feel I'm taking over her home." Allie paused briefly before asking, "Does Saloma have any close friends?"

Lydia reluctantly concluded, "*Nee*, I don't think so. Maybe when they were younger, Catherine Weaver and she were friends. But if I remember correctly, something happened around the time the bishop's *schwester* jumped the fence, putting a wedge between them. Never heard what it was, though. Why do you ask?"

"I was thinking if I could get some of her friends to visit, it might help her recover. The sooner she can take care of herself, the sooner Reuben and I can move back into the *doddi haus*."

"She's not always been the most welcoming regarding visitors, but I'll do my best to help. Let me talk to the women from the *g'may*. We can help carry some of the burden for you. Or at least give you a break every so often."

"Thank you." In a solemn tone, Allie resumed, "I'm not sure why *Gott* is pressing on me to take care of her when everyone knows she doesn't like me."

In a calm-spoken manner, Lydia added, "We all tend to like a safe *Gott* who doesn't ask too much of us. But trusting *Gott* requires letting go of our desire for control, especially when things don't make sense."

Lydia's words hung over her like a dark cloud, and she didn't know how to respond, let alone fully comprehend the message her mature friend was trying to share. All she knew was she was in for the storm of her life...she could feel it.

***

At noon, Almer and Reuben returned from town with Saloma in tow. She was noticeably thinner and frail-looking, something Allie hadn't expected, and it caught her off guard. Even Daniel sighed a little when he caught sight of her.

241

Her body was angled in an unnatural posture as Reuben led her to the chair before the window. "We set up weekly visits with a physical and occupational therapist who will come help her with speech and regaining the use of her arm. They advised us to keep her as active as possible, have a healthy, low-salt diet, and limit the sweets. Lots of rest and no…" Turning to Allie with a half-slanted smile, he emphasized, "Stress."

Trying to control the scowl that edged to her forehead, Allie mumbled, "Of course."

Carrying a bag of soiled clothes and used medical supplies to the bedroom, Allie sucked in a long breath to calm her anxious heart. She knew better than to think Reuben blamed her for his mother's condition, but his words hurt, to say the least.

After returning to the kitchen, she tucked a lap blanket over Saloma. Almer had pulled a chair beside his *datt* and asked him about the box they'd been looking for.

"I'm sorry to bother you, but Bishop Weaver and the other men are anxious to get this loan tied up before Mercer and his thugs call again."

He lowered his voice and directed the boys upstairs to a loose floorboard under the bed. Almer took the stairs two at a time while Reuben asked his father questions about the evidence.

"The men are hopeful you have enough to stop the balloon payment."

"Oh, it's enough. One call to Detective Powers, and this whole nonsense could be over. My plans were to avoid involving the sheriff but to handle it on our own. I have proof that they pulled this bait and switch scheme to a group of Amish farmers in the neighboring community a couple of years ago. When I followed the foreclosed land sale transfer, they all led back to Curtman. He's been putting all the Amish produce farmers out of business for over five years. The clincher is he's been using Mercer Lending as the frontman. But Mercer has a criminal record that will throw him back in jail if the right people get word of his involvement."

Reuben scratched his head and straddled a chair backward. "Do you really think showing him what we know will stop the loan?"

"We're still going to pay it back; we stand by our debt, but what it will do is stop the foreclosure. The balloon payment was something other than what we agreed to, and they altered the loan after we signed it. That's what's going to throw Mercer back in jail."

Almer stopped at their side with the empty tin box. "I found the box, but there's nothing in it."

"What do you mean it's empty? I left the papers in there. I'm sure of it."

Reuben lowered his voice after looking over at Allie and his mother. "*Mamm* said someone had been in the house after she got home from the hospital the day you got hurt. Could someone have found it?"

Almer piped in. "*Nee*, it was the bishop remember? And he didn't find a thing."

Reuben's father's eyes looked stricken, and his cheeks turned stark white. "*Gott* help us."

Almer shut the box and set it on the table. "We best go tell Mose and the others."

Trying to hear what the men were discussing as well as taking care of Saloma's comfort, Allie brushed her matted hair. As she twisted it up in a fresh bun and secured it under a clean *kapp,* she noticed a glimmer of gratitude in her mother-in-law's eyes. They glistened with an unceasing wish to cry, but all she could do was stare back at Allie, acting as if she wanted her to understand her feelings. At that moment, Allie's heart softened as Saloma turned to look aimlessly out the window.

Reuben took her hand and dragged her to the front room. "Will you be okay? Almer and I need to go to Bishop Weaver's."

With a wave and a thin smile, Allie replied, "Go, I'll be fine. I'll keep a careful eye on her." She hesitated momentarily. "I don't think she's going to give me any problem. And besides, it sounds like you and Almer have bigger issues to deal with. I'll take care of your parents. You go save the farm."

He wrapped his arms around her middle and rested his chin on her head. "How did I get so lucky?"

"Luck has nothing to do with it. I was just irresistible."

After pulling away, he kissed the tip of her nose and whispered a few unmentionable words in her ear, leaving her blushing at his boldness. She teased back. "I'll be waiting."

CHAPTER 15

Allie breathed deeply of the crisp November air. To her left, row after row of apple trees, barren of fruit and starting their descent into hibernation, and to her right, a world of possibilities for Raber Farms waiting to be unleashed.

After cleaning up the kitchen and helping Saloma with a shower, Allie left her in-laws a few minutes to themselves as she left with a pad and pencil. Pulling her jacket tight and tucking her dress behind her knees, she took residence on a fallen log. She let the sun warm her shoulders and looked at the open field. As far as she could see, only a few trees that lined the woods' edge had any remnants of color remaining, reminding her winter was soon to fall.

Turning to the notebook, she didn't hear Reuben approaching and jumped when he called her name. Shading her eyes, she scolded, "For heaven's sake, you could have warmed me before scaring the wits out of me."

"The snow helped me sneak up on you. I love it when you're startled. Your eyes become as wide as a newborn calf's."

She brushed the snow off the log and invited him to join her. "Did you follow me? I thought you were going to work at the furniture shop today."

"*Jah,* so did I, but I can't escape this farm. We get one thing fixed, and something else breaks down. Things are in such disarray. My carpentry skills come in handier around here than I ever imagined."

He pulled her in tight. "I couldn't help myself. When I saw you walk around the barn, I had to follow no matter how much work beckoned me." He sighed and looked back from where he came. "I shouldn't stay away too long."

"Trust me, they all did without you this long; the world won't end if you spend a few minutes with me." She cleared her throat and secured her notebook. "I love it out here."

"Me too. I spent all my spare time here on this ridge as a *kinner.*"

"And what did you do?" she asked.

"Boy stuff. Climbed trees, built forts, and chopped down this tree we're sitting on with a homemade axe. I wanted to be the next Daniel Boone and live in a cabin in the woods." He grinned and added, "That was until dinner time came and *Mamm's* apple cobbler called my name."

Allie stifled a smile. "I can't see you living off the land all alone. Where would you buy new books and enjoy a fancy coffee?"

"Exactly," he piped in. Stopping to kick off a clump of mud from his boots, he lowered his voice and leaned in closer. "And one thing I choose never to repeat is smoking my *datt's* pipe." Allie gave him a wide grin and exclaimed, "I'm certainly happy about that. I cringe every time your *datt* picks his up."

"*Jah*, smoking isn't my thing. Threw up for almost an hour after that stupid stunt. Elwin and Almer got a big kick at how green and pasty I got. They went and hid me in the barn until my color returned."

She giggled and waited for him to continue.

"What about you? What kind of trouble did you get yourself into?"

She crossed her legs and balanced her elbow on her knee, resting her chin in her palm. "Not much. I feared my dad, so I didn't get into too much trouble. However, we put a couple of drops of hot sauce in my dad's toothpaste once." She laughed, then exclaimed. "We never did tell him what we had done. He returned the container to the drugstore and demanded his money back."

They sat silently for the next few minutes, enjoying each other's company. When a plane flew overhead, Allie asked, "Did you ever wish to travel?"

"Where would I go?"

"Oh, I don't know anywhere, I guess. Maybe Ireland or Italy."

"Why would I want to go there?"

She elbowed his side. "For adventure, silly. To see how the rest of the world lives."

His jaw tightened visibly, and she commented, "I take it you have no desire to travel too far from home?"

He leaned his elbows on his knees. "I went all the way to Florida, didn't I?"

"That doesn't count. Anyone can go there." She got starry-eyed and added, "I mean somewhere different. Someplace beautiful. Anywhere we can try new foods and explore different cultures. You know, like Rome or Venice. I'd even settle for

West Ireland. I've read it's one of the prettiest places in the world."

With a reassuring touch of his hand, he stated, "You do know we aren't permitted to travel by plane."

Allie nodded, being reminded of the *Ordnung* restrictions. Traveling with her missionary parents gave her a sense of adventure, and she hadn't thought about what it might mean for future travel plans when she chose to marry Reuben and adopt his Amish culture.

Reuben's sudden shift in posture signaled he was trying to soften her shattered dreams and whispered, "I have everything I need right here with you. I don't need to see the rest of the world. You are my world and the prettiest thing I've ever seen. Why would I need to see anything else? I have the best of it all right here in front of me."

Internally, she pined. He certainly had a way of making her mold like clay in a potter's hand. "You're right. I don't need anything else either."

She laid her head on his shoulder and inhaled his woodsy scent. Digging her teeth into her bottom lip, she hoped to fight off emerging tears. Maybe it was the stress of caring for his parents or being with child, but her emotions were teetering firm to the surface all day. His reminder of the lack of adventure made her nose burn with disappointment. The mere thought of her child not seeing the world like she had left a massive hole in her heart. But the rush of emotions likely had more to do with a letter from Saloma's cousin she'd found tucked in a magazine. There was no mistake that the two women were discussing Reuben's choice in women…her, to be exact. The words…*Too many differences. I tell you, trouble*…etched thick in her memory and instantly surfaced with Reuben's reminder of the rules, which he expected her to abide by.

Reuben stood and held out his hand. "I best get back to the boys. Come on, I'll walk you back to the *haus*."

Letting the warmth of his hand mingle in hers, she walked in step with him through the field. When the clearing she had been admiring earlier came into view, she stopped. "I've been thinking…"

"Oh no… that's never a good thing," he joked.

She slapped his arm. "No, really, I'm serious." Waving her hand to point out the slight rise in the landscape, she kept on, "I think this would be the perfect spot to build a house. It faces northeast, and we could enjoy warm sunrises in the morning and be shielded from the afternoon sun in the evenings. If you agree, we could add a porch to the back of the house to take in those sunsets." She held her breath, waiting for his response.

He uttered a curt grunt. "Why would we go to the expense of building a *haus*? I'm the youngest and will get the main farm someday. We'd stay in the *doddi haus* until *Mamm* and *Datt* were ready to slow down some."

Without stopping her voice from rising an octave, she replied, "The *doddi haus*? It's so small. How can we raise a family there? It only has two bedrooms. Furthermore, I thought your *mamm* took that away since you wouldn't work on the farm. Have you changed your mind about going back to woodworking?"

He pulled her hand up under his elbow. "I've thought that I'd like to help my *bruders* build back up the farm. *Datt* said he has some ideas about increasing our profits." Reuben patted her hand. "If we can take care of this loan, we can start looking toward the future. I think I want to be part of that."

Allie drew her hand away. "Why didn't you discuss this with me?"

"I am. Right now."

Her voice, tight with emotion, shouted, "No, it sounds like you've already decided. You should have discussed it with me first since it involves both of us."

"Calm down. You're overreacting."

"Overreacting! I'm doing no such thing. You're forgetting you're married now, and we're to make decisions like this together."

He moved closer, picked up her chin with his thumb, and uttered, "And you're forgetting I'm the head of this family and have every right to make choices that I feel are best for our family."

Big, round tears spilled over her bottom lashes as she studied his face. Confusion, disappointment, and a wave of nausea forced her to brush his hand away and run toward the house.

Their first honest disagreement left her bewildered to the point of exhaustion. Instead of checking on Daniel and Saloma, she ran to her room and threw herself across their bed. She cried until the tears dried up, and sleep overtook her.

***

A chill passed over Allie's skin as she opened her eyes. Afternoon had turned into night, and she heard mumbled voices in the kitchen below. The smell of roasting chicken seeped under the shut door, and guilt forced her to jump out of bed. Someone had started dinner without waking her. The thought of Daniel having to care for Saloma all afternoon by himself dug a sliver of remorse through her chest. Wiping the sleep from her eyes and pushing out the wrinkles from her paisley-printed dress, she strained to distinguish the voices as she slipped back on her shoes.

Stopping at the top of the stairs, she listened as Daniel explained all her considerations for Raber Farms to Reuben and his *bruders*. Her father-in-law's words stung. "I suggest we take it slow. Develop a plan and incorporate one new element each year. We should have a fully operational destination venue by the end of five years."

Reuben excitedly stated, "*Datt*, this is such a great idea. How did you come up with this?"

With his answer, Allie sank to the top step. "I've had lots of time to ponder how we could bring Raber Farms back to life."

A sob lodged in Allie's throat, and she had to cover her mouth to keep it from revealing her hiding spot.

"We should eventually work toward converting the big barn into a space that can be rented out for weddings and such. Even offering it out for the *Englisch*."

Almer questioned. "Weddings? Will the bishop approve?"

"If I can show him the numbers and prove that it will help support the community and not infringe on our beliefs, I think we could get special approval."

Reuben added, "So let me get this straight. You want us to completely revamp the barn by adding a catering kitchen, grow Christmas trees for the *Englisch*, offer sleigh and hayrides, plant pumpkins, open a gift shop highlighting Amish products, and you want to go as far as planting a corn maze next year?"

"*Jah*, you got it."

Almer slapped his father on the back. "I'm impressed. I never dreamed you'd come up with such a harebrained idea. But I like it."

In a broad German accent, Daniel added, "But it's all contingent on getting this loan paid first."

Allie watched as Reuben turned a chair around and straddled it. "How do you suggest we do that? You've been trying to catch us up for almost a year now with little success."

A commotion of voices sounded as all the boys added their two cents without a concrete plan.

Daniel tapped his pipe on the table. "I have an idea concerning that as well. As soon as we locate my missing proof and only after we see if threatening Mercer and Curtman works, we can gather the bishop and the men from the community and present our plans. I'm thinking we could sell shares of Raber Farms. That would give our Amish community a vested interest in the project and help fund our building project. If we succeed, so will they. It's sure to pass approval then."

A hollow left-out feeling forced Allie to move back to her room quietly. Everything she and Daniel had spoken about the last few weeks was laid out as if he had come up with them himself. No credit was given to her, and she felt betrayed by the one man whom she felt was on her side. No matter how hard she tried, she'd never be accepted by anyone in the Raber family, and she didn't think she could conform to the Amish way of life.

Crawling back into bed, she pulled the blankets over her head and cried, "Lord, what have I gotten myself into? I've made a terrible mistake."

***

It was all Allie could do to crawl out of bed the following day and face the world. Even after Reuben came to bed, she pretended to be sleeping, ignoring his gentle nudges to snuggle tight. She was still realizing that she held little hope in having a voice in her marriage and the Raber family. Her only saving grace now was that Saloma still had not regained her voice.

Rolling to the side of the bed, she tried to push back the blankets without waking Reuben. She sighed when he reached for her and allowed him to pull her closer. Burying his nose in the back of her head, he asked, "Are you feeling okay? You never came down for dinner last night."

"*Jah*, I was tired, is all."

"And now? Are you feeling rested?"

"I suppose." Removing his arm from her middle, she moved to the edge of the bed. "I need to start breakfast and check on your parents."

He reached for her again. "It's early. I'm sure they can wait a few more minutes."

Wiggling from his grip, she stood and dressed for the day. Lighting the small oil lamp on her dresser, she noticed a new navy-blue dress and white *kapp* hanging on the peg by the door. "Where did those come from?"

"Almer's *fraa* brought them by last night."

"For what?"

"I assumed you asked for them. I didn't question her. I just told her I would give them to you."

With a defiant tone, she replied, "There is nothing wrong with the dresses I have."

Reuben pulled himself up to a sitting position. "I'm sure she meant nothing by it." Rubbing sleep from his eyes, he said. "Perhaps she just wanted to be nice. Did you consider that?"

Allie held the dress up to examine it more closely. "It's a maternity dress. I'm certainly nowhere close to needing it." She held up the *kapp*. "And what am I supposed to do with this? My lace covering suits me just fine."

Reuben moved to her side. "Don't get all worked up. I'm sure it was a gift and nothing else."

Still looking for an underlying motive, Allie asked, "Is this what you want me to wear?" When he didn't answer immediately but took both the dress and kapp and hung them on the peg, she snapped, "One more thing that you've failed to discuss with me first."

"Why are you so testy this morning?"

"You didn't answer me. Do you want me to dress more in line with your family?"

He pulled her close, tipped her chin up, and studied her eyes. "I want you to do whatever makes you happy. We haven't decided what church we'll join yet, so until then, you wear what you're comfortable in."

"And if I don't want to join the Amish church?"

A forlorn look fell to his face, and a surge of regret landed heavily on her chest. "Well, at least the Old Order church," she said hesitantly.

His stance stiffened slightly. "I can promise you it won't be that one. But I do want us to try the New Order Fellowship on Sunday." He moved to pull fresh clothes from the dresser. "It will still be a change from what you're accustomed to, but I'm praying it'll be a good place for both of us. Besides, there are more younger families there that we might connect with better."

After slipping on his pants, he kissed her head and whispered, "If I haven't told you, thank you for caring for my parents."

Nodding and walking to the window after he left, she gazed out over the dim, gloomy, rain-filled morning. She felt alone and wiped a few fresh tears from her cheek.

She didn't hear him return, but suddenly, he was behind her, husky whispers in her ear. Although he didn't touch her, he was near enough that his breath fell on her skin. "I'm sorry for yesterday."

When she turned around, he cupped her face in his hands. "I've been spending too much time with my *bruders* and their Old Order way of handling family matters."

"I thought we were going to be different," she murmured, her heart still aching from their disagreement.

When their hands brushed together, he laced his fingers in hers; it felt completely natural. Swiftly, all her doubts disappeared and were instantly replaced with his warm declaration of love.

Tracy Fredrychowski

CHAPTER 16

M orning rain pattered against the kitchen window as Allie washed dishes. It had been a trying morning. Saloma was more than agitated at her limited state, and Daniel became incredibly bored. It took everything she had to escape their combined darkened moods and not add to their discomfort with her own.

Even though she and Reuben had cleared the air that morning, she couldn't help but harbor a twinge of hostility toward Daniel.

"Allie, come in here and figure out what Saloma requires."

Following her father-in-law's voice to the front room, she groaned internally at his request.

Saloma desperately tried to get up from her chair and wouldn't stop until Allie helped her stand. "What is it?"

The woman held her cane up and pointed to the bedroom off the living room. "Do you want to go lie down?"

She pounded her cane on the floor several times and shook her head, pointing again to the room. "Okay, then let me help you at least."

Saloma twisted until she took control of Allie's arm and grunted in disapproval. Biting down on her bottom lip, Allie steadied the woman's stance, preventing her from falling while hoping to control her building frustration.

"Perhaps we should be working on you being able to write your requests on paper. Your therapist requires you to work on communication skills."

The glare the woman threw her way landed profoundly on her cheek as she helped her sit on the edge of the bed. With her right arm lying limp against her side, Saloma used her other to point her cane around the room.

Resting her hands on her hips, Allie asked, "What? I don't know what you want."

It was disturbing watching the scene unfold. Clearly, Saloma was trying to get her to look for something, but the room was void of anything but the bed, dresser, and rocking chair. A few papers and magazines were stacked on the nightstand, and an array of medicine bottles on top of the dresser. Just the day before, she had cleaned the room while they were napping in their chairs.

Opening the drawers, she sifted through each one, showing her that nothing was inside but the clean clothes she had placed there the day before. Stomping her cane on the floor, Saloma got her attention and pointed to the drawer on the nightstand.

"There's nothing in here but a notepad and a few pens. What are you looking for?"

Letting the cane slide to the floor, Saloma took her left hand and ran it along the front of her nightdress repeatedly.

Exasperated beyond words, Allie sat on the bed and handed her a pen. "You'll have to learn to write with your left hand. We're not getting anywhere like this."

Just as Saloma took the pen from her hand and Allie balanced the notepad on her knee, Reuben's voice thundered from the front room.

"The whole batch is ruined. Someone added a whole bag of rock salt to the vat."

"Rock salt? What are you talking about?" Daniel demanded.

"I'm telling you, *Datt*, someone is trying to ruin us, and I can only bet it has something to do with Mercer and his thugs."

Tugging on Allie's arm, Saloma nodded her head toward the front room. After helping her back to her feet, both women followed the voices into the other room. As she held the rocking chair for Saloma to settle back into, Allie asked, "Reuben, are you sure?"

"Oh, I'm certain. I found the empty bag hidden behind a crate of apples."

"Could it have been an accident?"

"Hardly, it was deliberate. We don't add anything to our cider."

Allie tilted her head up and followed a smell with her nose. "What is that? Are you burning something?"

Reuben moved to the window, and Allie followed. She gasped, and he took off running out the front door, leaving it open on his way out. Through the light rain, bellows of smoke rolled out of the barn mixed with fire shards. Her eyes stared far beyond the barn and caught sight of two men running down the lane.

Standing aside for Daniel to see out the door, she hollered, "Look there, *Datt,* do you see them?"

A hopeless, grief-stricken look on her father-in-law's face focused on where she pointed, and he moaned, "*Englischers.*"

An eerie sensation filled the room as he retreated to some dark closet in his mind. He said nothing as she ran from the *haus* to the office to call 911.

The ground shook as the diesel fuel tank exploded at the side of the cider barn. Moments later, the barn was fully engulfed in flames. Pulling herself back up from the ground, she ran toward the office. It all seemed blurred and unreal as she dialed for help.

The fire trucks and neighbors came immediately, but nothing could be done to save the old structure. The firemen worked on saving the storage barn and office instead.

The heat from the fire did little to warm her tattered soul, but someone handed her a jacket to cover her rain-soaked dress. Even nature couldn't save generations of work.

Finally, Reuben found her in the crowd and stood behind her as they watched the firemen extinguish the last smoldering hot spots. The hundred-year-old barn lay in ruins, along with the Raber family's blood, sweat, and tears. Utter destruction lingered in the air as the family stood in total shock.

The fire chief walked up beside Reuben and his *bruders*. "The fire appears to have started near the engine used to power the cider press. From there, it ignited the diesel tank. There was no saving the barn once that exploded."

Allie tried to interrupt the fire chief by explaining what she saw before the tank exploded, but Reuben instantly hushed her.

It wasn't until the man walked away that he turned to Almer and squeezed Allie's hand, urging her to release what she'd been dying to say.

"Almer, I saw two *Englisch* men run out from behind the barn."

His long, helpless, irritated face nodded. "*Jah*, we saw them too."

Allie pleaded, "Shouldn't we tell someone?"

Reuben and Almer hung their heads in silent despair, but Almer responded, "Oh, we're going to tell someone, but it will be on our terms for sure and certain."

Reuben bent and whispered close to her ear, "Please go inside out of the rain and check on *Mamm* and *Datt*. We need to talk to the bishop and some of the men."

She shook from the cold and was anxious to get out of her wet clothes. If it weren't for Catherine Weaver, who volunteered to sit with Saloma and Daniel, she would have been forced inside earlier.

Back in the house, Catherine handed her a dry towel. "Go change out of those wet things, and I'll make you hot tea."

Wiping soot off her face and nodding toward the front room, she asked, "How are they?"

Lowering her voice, the elderly woman muttered, "I think they're in shock. I tried to soothe them as best as I could."

"I'll change and be right back. Thank you for sitting with them."

Catherine shook her head. "What a shame. Just one thing after another, not sure how much more they can take."

Catherine took her coat off the peg. "Let me go tell them I'm leaving, and I'll be back soon."

Allie removed her wet sweater and watched as Catherine leaned in and whispered something in Saloma's ear. When she did, Saloma cringed in the most disturbing manner, leaving Allie wondering what she might have said.

***

People moved in and out of the house for the next few hours, dropping off food and planning to return in a few days to begin the cleanup. With each visitor, Saloma became increasingly anxious, to the point that Allie led her to the bedroom, leaving the stress of the day behind them.

Something seemed to turn and break inside Saloma when Allie helped her into bed. Catching her hand with her good arm, Saloma clutched Allie's hand and squeezed. A wide-eyed look of fear gripped the woman's eyes, and Allie sat on the side of the bed. There was no way of knowing what was happening inside her head, but the lone tear that rolled down her cheek told Allie all she needed. There was no fight left inside of Saloma Raber.

She didn't know how long she sat and held her mother-in-law's hand, but she waited until her breathing became steady before leaving.

Daniel didn't argue as she helped him to his feet and led him into the bedroom. An array of mumbled voices resonated on the front porch, and she wondered why they didn't include Daniel in their conversation. He hadn't uttered a word since she'd come inside, and he remained disengaged, which worried her more than anything else.

He handed her his crutches as he wiggled out of his broadcloth trousers and sat on the side of the bed. Typically, Reuben helped his father dress for bed, but at that moment, he didn't flinch when she put his feet through pajama bottoms and pulled him to a standing position to pull them up. His body weight shifted slightly as his shoulders sank in a defeated state.

Helping him lower back to the bed, she removed his shirt and guided his arms through the matching top. When he didn't move to button it, she patiently responded without a word. There wasn't the faintest flicker of interest in helping himself, so she lifted his legs to the bed and tucked the quilt under his chin. He instantly shut his eyes, and she turned down the oil lamp and left.

Allie leaned on the closed door and exhaled as she looked around the room. Wet towels and tracked-in mud covered the room's hardwood floor. The men were still crowded under the porch's roof in a heated conversation, one of which she had no desire to be part of.

She picked up a few more towels from the kitchen and carried the armful to the basement. A stench filled every ounce of air, reminding her that her family's livelihood had gone up in smoke in a matter of minutes.

The apple storage barn was full and now ruined, along with the cider mill. Any likelihood of settling their outstanding loan before the end of the year was also gone. Unless someone could devise a plan quickly, foreclosure would be their only option.

A morbid moodiness befell her, much like Saloma and Daniel, and she understood their sense of defeat. Suddenly, she felt the pain of their loss. She hadn't felt like a part of the family before, but the realization forced her to sit on the bottom of the basement stairs and weep. All alone, she cried out to the Lord to help her make sense of the misfortune that seemed to be hanging over her family. From somewhere deep, she heard in her mind, *Stop looking in the past; if you don't, you'll miss what I have planned for your future.*

Wiping tears from her face, she carried the armload of towels to the washer, dropping one to the floor. When she bent to retrieve it, she noticed one of Saloma's aprons lying behind the wringer washer. When she picked it up, papers fell from the pocket. Tears sprang to her eyes as she ran upstairs and out onto the porch. In unison, the men sighed in relief when she handed Reuben the proof they sought.

***

The air was still heavy with smoke as the sun burned the mist from the charred remains of the Raber farm. Allie covered her nose as she walked past the barn. Reuben and his *bruders* were already out assessing the damage and cleaning up what they could while waiting for the embers to burn out.

Returning a dish to Lydia, she found her working on repotting a couple of mums on her front porch. After setting the bowl on the railing, Allie sat on the small bench near the front door.

Lydia shook her head. "Such a shame." The aged woman brushed soil from her hands and sat beside her. "Any word on how the fire started?"

With a forlorn little nod, Allie replied, "The fire chief said they are sending a fire marshal out today, but his initial opinion is it was started around the diesel engine that runs the cider press."

"You don't sound so sure."

"Reuben and Almer think it was started deliberately." In a sense of bewilderment, she added, "Please don't repeat that. They're unsure, and I'd hate to speak out of turn."

Lydia nodded with sadness. "How are Reuben's parents?"

"It was all I could do to get them to breakfast this morning. It took both Reuben and I to convince them to get out of bed. Daniel hasn't said a word, and that worries me."

"They'll bounce back, just give them some time, and I'll be praying for them."

"What if they don't?"

Lydia took her hand. "They will, especially with you taking care of them."

Allie laughed a nervous giggle. "I hardly think I'll have anything to do with it. I'm just a means to an end when caring for them. They had no one else, and I was elected."

Lydia smiled. "Don't be so sure of that. *Gott* put you exactly where he wanted you for this time in life. He has our paths laid out way before letting us in on his plans."

Lydia paused and patted her hand. "He will give you everything you need to accomplish your purpose as His servant."

Allie sighed. "I've not had too much of a servant's heart through all this. Saloma is difficult and...Daniel..." She shook her head. "It doesn't matter; I'm doing all I can, I guess."

"I believe we reap what we sow, and *Gott* will reward you for your faithfulness," Lydia said consolingly.

"That's not encouraging," Allie breathed.

"Why not?"

"If we reap what we sow, I'm afraid I'll have a pile of rocks instead of fruitful trees."

"Now, Allie, take your time to judge your actions. When it comes to cultivating, it takes a lot of hard work to prepare the soil, plant the seed, water its growth, and protect it from storms. Reaping only comes after the end of a long, difficult process called life."

"And that applies to my life how?"

"Oh, child, you've just started to plant those seeds. When you get as old as me, you will have had hundreds of gardens you've tended to. Hurt feelings, bitterness, and anger will be like those weeds and rocks you've thrown from your garden. And believe me, all the work is exhausting, but in the end, *Gott* will reward you with soft, pliable soil to plant seeds that will produce good fruit."

Allie tried to smile, but it came out as a grimace. "It all sounds too hard."

Lydia grinned and waited a few moments before asking, "What would you do if *Gott* showed up on your front step and said, "'Follow me?'"

Without hesitation, she replied, "I'd follow him."

"Of course, you would. And what would happen if he placed you in the middle of a garden and told you he wanted you to work the soil by pulling weeds and carrying the rocks to the garden's edge?"

Allie didn't answer but pondered Lydia's analogy.

Lydia continued. "If that was your assignment, would you question Him?"

In an almost melancholy emotion, Allie replied, "I would hope I would get back to work pulling weeds."

Lydia's smile widened. "Exactly. That's what you're doing by caring for Saloma and Daniel. You are cultivating the soil for future generations of the Raber family. You're putting the time into laying a good foundation for a plentiful harvest later down the road."

Allie grunted. "Lydia, you know you're talking about Saloma. Are you certain she'll change, even after she gets her voice back?"

Lydia wrapped her arm around Allie's shoulders and pulled her close. "I bet your mother-in-law has had much time to consider her actions. I can almost bet this experience will change her. I don't see how it won't."

Allie leaned into her friend's embrace. "My faith will certainly be renewed if my labor is not all in vain."

"Trust me, Allie, the more time and energy we put into loving our families now, the more we will understand *Gott's* desire for our lives in the future."

"I sure hope you're right because loving a family who doesn't love me is hard."

"Give them time to get to know you like I do. They will see your big heart and how much you have to give."

Allie pushed the wrinkles out of her apron and pulled her sweater tight. "I best get back; Reuben will be wanting dinner soon." Standing and stopping at the top step, she added, "Thank you for knowing exactly what I need to hear."

Lydia smiled. "*Gott* knew what he was doing when he placed me in your path. When I was younger, I had a mature woman who would encourage me. Much like I hope I do for you."

Allie moved closer and hugged Lydia again. "You have no idea what it means to me."

"I do because I knew what it meant when my friend could breathe life into almost any situation I struggled with. Sometimes, it just takes someone with fresh eyes to point out the obvious."

Allie practically skipped down the steps and went back home. Lydia put a fresh new spin on her role in the Raber family. Regardless, if Saloma never came to enjoy her company, or if Daniel took all the credit for her ideas, she was right where *Gott* had placed her, and she wouldn't question His purpose for her life again.

CHAPTER 17

After dinner, Reuben helped his parents to their chairs in the living room, and Allie cleaned up the kitchen. Reuben invited her for an evening stroll, and she was looking forward to some alone time with her husband. Knowing how they had struggled lately, she felt Reuben had something to discuss with her by the way he rushed through his meal.

Mose and Catherine Weaver had arrived shortly after supper and were visiting with Saloma and Daniel. Even though Catherine gave Allie reason to pause, she appreciated their visit, allowing her to spend extra time with Reuben.

She stepped outside, taking her heavy shawl from the peg by the door, and marveled at the crescent moon rising in the sky. The air still had a pungent edge of destruction, and she tried to ignore its offensive odor by picking up on the lingering perfume of burning leaves. As Allie made her way around the side of the *haus*, one of the barn cats ran in her path, chasing a mouse under the porch, and she stepped aside, letting out a slight squeal. "Eek!" Grabbing onto Reuben's arm. "I like that they keep the mice away, but they sure do think they own the place."

"Everyone has a job around here, and if they expect to stay, they have to pay their way," Reuben said with a rueful smile.

Looping her arm in his, she asked, "Does that include me?"

He squeezed her hand without answering. They were quiet for a few minutes, taking in the way the moonlight changed the burnt rumble of the barn into a soft sculpture. After a while, he said, "*Datt's* notions for the farm were yours."

She knew exactly what he was referring to. "I just…wanted to help, so I came up with some ideas to help breathe some life back into Raber Farms."

She stopped and turned to face him. "What? Why are you looking at me like that? Are you upset I put my two cents in where I clearly didn't belong?"

He let out a hearty laugh. "Allie Raber not speak her mind, fat chance of that ever happening."

For a split second, she couldn't tell if he was mad or elated, but as soon as she held her flashlight under his chin to reveal his catty smile, she had her answer. "You have a heart of gold, Allie," he said. "Always thinking of everyone else." He took his index finger and softly tapped her chest over her heart. "It's one of the reasons I married you."

His words softened the worry lines around her eyes. "Really? You're not mad I stepped into your father's business like I did?"

"Mad? Goodness no. I knew the minute *Datt* started to outline his ideas that they were yours. He has some great ideas but has yet to come up with anything like that. Even Almer commented on how it was unlike he'd ever heard come out of *Datt's* mouth."

They continued their walk around the perimeter of the burnt barn and cider mill. "I'm worried about your parents."

"As we all are. We've never seen *Datt* so detached. He's half the reason I encouraged the bishop to visit with them this evening. They've been friends for a long time."

Allie sighed and tilted her head back to look at the stars. "What's Catherine's story? I didn't think your mother and her were very close."

"I think they were at one time. But something happened to put a strain on their relationship, and I don't think they ever sprang back."

"I can't get your *mamm* to work on her communication skills. Her therapist wants her to learn how to write with her left hand, but she gets agitated whenever I try to encourage her. Just this morning, she brushed the pad and pencil to the floor in defiance. I find it difficult to understand what she needs me to do…if anything."

"Not everyone could deal with her, especially after what she's put you through. It takes a big person to be so nice after all that."

They walked hand in hand, and Allie stated, "I'm definitely not as nice as you think I am." She took her free hand and wrapped her fingers around Reuben's forearm. "Tolerable is more like it."

"Whatever you call it, I appreciate your loyalty."

"What choice did I have? It's not like she has much of a family willing to step up."

"She does now," he said.

"Does now what?" she asked.

"Have a family willing to step up." Reuben steadied her hand as they stepped over a pile of debris. "She has many sons, and not one of their *fraas* stepped forward. I'd say that says something about your character, and I'll be sure to point it out."

Allie wondered if it was the right time to let Reuben know how she was feeling and walked silently for a few minutes as she pondered her words.

She gave a slight shiver, and he pulled her close. "Cold?"

"A little, but I'm not ready to go back inside. I'm quite enjoying our walk."

He slid his arm around her waist and brought her into his chest so close, his warm breath tickled her ear. "I know how to warm you up," he whispered.

She stepped back and giggled. "I'm sure you do, but I want to discuss something first."

"Uh-oh, I'm in trouble now!"

She shooed away his arm. "No, you're not. I want to let you know I don't feel like a part of your family. I think everyone tolerates me, and they don't take me seriously. Especially the way your *datt* scooted around the truth about the ideas for the farm."

Reuben braced to look in her eyes and held the flashlight under her chin. "Mrs. Raber, you have it all wrong. Almer and the rest of my *bruders* are very grateful you came along. They're not stupid and know exactly the sacrifices you're making...." He shined the light on the ground. "What's that?"

They both followed the light to the glare of something shiny, half buried in the mud. Allie stooped and picked up the piece of metal. "It's a brass button."

Reuben wiped the dirt away. "It looks new. I've never seen anything like it before. Can't say anyone around here would have anything like this."

Allie took the flashlight from Reuben's hand and pointed it closer. "It's not Amish, for sure."

"Too fancy for anything one of the firefighters might have had on," he asserted.

***

Mose sat in the chair across from Daniel and stated, "There's a special bond that forms between men who've gone through what we have." Daniel glanced away. "I know you understand what I'm talking about so don't ignore me. We know more about each other than we're willing to admit."

Catherine flipped her *kapp* strings over her shoulders and leaned closer to Saloma. "Mose told me what you've been threatening him with, and I'm pleading with you to drop it." Her voice cracked. "You have no idea what trouble you'll stir up if you divulge the truth. You'll not only hurt our family but our sons too."

With her declaration, Daniel finally sputtered, "Quit badgering her. Can't you see the poor woman no longer has a voice? She may never regain her speech at this rate, so you have nothing to worry about."

"Calm down, Daniel; we didn't come to upset you or Saloma. We came as friends, first and foremost," Mose stated humbly.

Catherine addressed her husband. "I feel bad you must deal with this in the middle of everything else."

Mose shook his head. "I know my duties both as husband and district leader. This issue is no different from the next."

"Can't this wait?" Daniel asked defiantly. "My family's livelihood was just lost, and you want to talk about Saloma's idle threats." He repositioned himself and rubbed the pain from his leg. "I wouldn't have allowed her to carry out her threats."

Mose crossed his arms over his chest and leaned back in his chair. "I would hope not, but I need to ensure that's where they stay…just idle threats."

Daniel cleared his throat. "I've had lots of time to sit in this chair and think about things. And while I've been blessed in ways I cannot begin to appreciate; I've learned that life doesn't always give us what we want."

Mose added, "*Nee*, it gives us what we need, whether we want it or not."

"Much like giving us a son long after we had given up any ability of having our own child," Catherine replied shyly.

Catherine caught Mose's eye. "Before that, we would never have dreamed of wading through the muck of secrets and what they could do to a family if ever exposed."

Mose looked at Catherine. "She wanted children so badly," he said. "We tried to adopt, but all those years ago, releasing *Englisch* children to an Amish family was unheard of. Too many differences, they said."

"What does it matter now?" Daniel groaned.

Catherine turned to face Saloma. "We were friends, and you knew how badly I wanted children."

Saloma turned her face away, and Catherine continued to address her. "When Mose's *schwester* was brutally attacked and found herself with child, it was finally our chance for a child. We never told anyone, not even our parents. She moved away, and I went with her until she delivered."

Catherine stifled a sob. "I don't understand how you felt you could use that against us when a child meant so much to me." Saloma pulled away when Catherine laid her hand on her arm. "I thought we were friends."

"My *schwester* went on to marry an *Englischer*, but she was never the same after that attack," Mose said bluntly. He paused, took off his glasses, and pinched the bridge of his nose. "Our boy doesn't know. We raised him with all the love and support like he was our flesh and blood." He polished his glasses on his shirt sleeve. "I suppose we tempted fate by never revealing the truth to the boy."

Catherine faced Saloma and finished lamely, "Then you came along and wanted to upset everything we had worked so hard to conceal."

Before Daniel could comment, Reuben and Allie walked in the front door. "Look what we found!" Reuben exclaimed as he held the button out to his father and Mose.

"Where did you find that?" Mose asked.

"Between the barn and the diesel tank."

Daniel held his hand out, and Reuben dropped it into his open palm. Reuben glanced at Allie at his father's request and said, "Unless Mercer and his band of thugs are now employing women, I find this a crucial piece of how the fire started."

Mose took the button from Daniel. "I'll keep it. We have plans to confront Mercer and Curtman tomorrow. I might need it for more leverage."

A stifling stillness filled the air, and Catherine cleared her throat. "I'm getting tired, Mose. Can we go?"

Once outside, the moon had slid behind the clouds, and Catherine had to hold on to Mose as they made their way to their buggy. Walking close with their heads low, Catherine whispered, "I've seen that button."

"So have I."

They barely said a word on the ride home, and Catherine only groaned an acknowledgment of their dilemma when Mose stopped on the covered bridge to throw the button in the creek.

***

The men huddled in Mose's barn out of the icy rain as they discussed their plan to confront Mercer. The bishop had sent word to both Curtman and Mercer to meet them that morning.

Almer held his father's research up and shook it in the air. "We have everything we need to prove we're serious about going to the officials if they don't waive the December 31st deadline."

Before anyone could comment, a black truck pulled up to the barn, and two men moved quickly through the rain. When the *Englischmen* stepped inside, Reuben couldn't help but notice one of the men wore a cavernous scar angling from his jaw down to the side of his neck. "This better be important," Mercer snarled.

Propping himself up on a haybale, his father replied threateningly, "Depends on how badly you want to end up back in prison."

Startled by his father's bluntness, Reuben balled his fists as the man moved quickly to Daniel's side. "I wouldn't be so quick to hurl warnings, old man. You have more to lose than we do."

Stepping back when Almer grabbed his arm, Reuben remembered that his mild-mannered father had a stealthy persona.

Earlier that morning, they had set a video recorder Almer had borrowed from one of their *Englisch* neighbors to capture their meeting. If they admitted to their bait and switch scheme, they would have all the proof necessary if his father's evidence wasn't enough.

"What's this all about?" Curtman demanded. "I assume you're prepared to pay the remaining balloon payment today."

Daniel snorted a response. "Over my dead body."

Mercer moved in close and pointed a finger at Daniel's chest. "That can be arranged."

Bishop Weaver stepped in the middle of the two men. "There will be none of that. We've called you here for a reason, and it has nothing to do with paying that payment."

Almer waved a manilla folder. "The truth can't be hidden forever."

Mercer tried to snatch the file, but Almer quickly pulled it to safety, adding, "The truth always prevails."

Reuben inserted, "Like setting fire to our barn and adding salt to the cider vat."

"All hearsay," Curtman spat. "You can think all you want, but we didn't have a thing to do with that."

"Mose, show them the button, it's clearly *Englisch*," Almer challenged.

The bishop grunted. "It's not relevant to this meeting."

Daniel stomped his crutch on the pine plank floor. "Boys, enough!" Holding his hand out to Almer, he said, "Give me that."

Something about how the bishop brushed off the button raised goosebumps on Reuben's skin. *He was sure that what they found was pertinent. Why wasn't Mose presenting it along with his father's findings?* he thought.

His father looked very serious as he shuffled through the papers, and Mercer showed his annoyance with a scowl. "Get on with it, man," Mercer's voice was rough with fury.

"We know what you've done to us and many of our Amish friends. And we're prepared to go to the authorities if we can't devise a compromise concerning our loan."

Despite his apprehension, Reuben felt a stab of pride at how his father stood up to both men. His voice didn't waver, and his stance was strong despite his limited capacity.

"I've been researching Curtman Produce and Mercer Lending for months and have all the proof we need."

"Give me that," Curtman insisted as he seized the documents. Curtman said nothing as he examined the proof. In a huff, he bellowed and turned toward Mercer. "You fool! You've left a paper trail a mile long." Throwing the papers to the floor, he charged Mercer and pushed him up against the wall. "I'll be ruined. You were supposed to dispose of them. They have it all: names, dates, deed transfers, and original loan documents."

"You'd better listen to me." Curtman grabbed the front of Mercer's shirt. "You don't scare me. I have more dirt on you than you do on me." Mercer tried to wrench away, but Curtman held fast.

"The District Attorney's Office will be interested in how you obtained those hefty tax breaks," Mercer spat back.

Mercer pushed him away with a sneering shove. Curtman stared at him, digesting his comment. "What?"

"You heard me. Don't think for one minute I'll go down alone. I watch my own back. I'll do whatever it takes and by any means necessary." He stopped momentarily and rubbed his balled-up knuckles over the scar on his face. "I'll take the fall for many things, but I won't end back up in the pen for anyone. Even if that includes divulging your under-the-table business deals to cut my own throat."

Mercer snapped free. "This is far from over, and it will take more than a few two-bit Amish farmers to lock me up again."

He brushed the dust from his hands and barked, "You best settle the loan. They go to the feds, and we both go under."

Curtman turned toward Daniel, his expression exuded anger and distress. "What will it take?"

There was a long pause, then Daniel stated, "We have no desire to default on the original loan. We pay our debts."

Curtman shrugged. "Then what?"

"We want all foreclosure proceedings halted," Daniel said stiffly.

Bishop Weaver handed Mercer a check with the balance of the loan. "And we want written notice that the loan is paid in full."

Reuben glanced at Almer, shrugged, and thought, *how on earth did he come up with that?*

Reuben couldn't keep quiet. "What about the fire, rat-infested apples, and ruined cider? We've lost so much; who'll pay for that?"

Mose gave him a serpent's stare. "We'll deal with that on our own."

Pondering the irony, Reuben kept his opinions to himself as he listened to his father and Bishop Weaver's details to release them from the dooming loan and foreclosure.

A vein in Curtman's temple throbbed, but otherwise, he stood motionless as Daniel and Mose outlined their terms. There was no doubt in Reuben's mind they had finally taken the lead, thanks to his father's evidence and the bishop's check.

A spray of wet snow and ice landed inside the open door as the two men sped off. Reuben noticed a sudden tightness around his father's mouth right before he inserted, "I doubt we've seen the last of them."

"I get the feeling Mercer doesn't like to lose," Almer piped in.

"Precisely why we're not pressing him on the fire and vandalism." The bishop pulled on his long gray beard. "Best we let sleeping dogs lie."

Reuben didn't like the look the two men exchanged and made a mental note to ask Almer about it.

"Guess we didn't need the video after all."

"Keep it anyway." Daniel pulled himself up on both crutches. "Like I said, I'm not convinced we've heard the last of this."

Reuben and Almer stayed back to take down the camera as the rest of the men dispersed. "Something's not right," Reuben whispered. "Did you see how *Datt* and Mose looked at each other when we mentioned the barn?"

"*Jah*. What are they keeping from us?"

"Your guess is as good as mine, but I don't like it one bit."

Sleet started to ping the ground as the young men stood in the doorway and watched Mose and their *datt* pull away. Almer pulled his hat snug and tucked the camera in his pocket. "We should have found a way to put this recorder in the bishop's buggy."

The men ducked through the icy rain toward Almer's buggy. "Where do you think they're going? I would have assumed *Datt* would have gotten a ride home with us." Reuben untethered his horse and climbed inside. "I don't like it one bit, and if Allie didn't have a doctor's appointment, we'd be following them."

Almer shook the rain from his black felt hat. "Let it be *bruder*. Maybe this time it's better we don't know what they're up to. We've got enough to worry about as it is."

"*Jah*, you're right.

Tracy Fredrychowski

CHAPTER 18

Allie put the finishing touches on dinner when Reuben appeared with Almer. "It's all settled!" Reuben exclaimed as he lifted the cover off the pot of chicken and dumplings.

"Where's your *datt*?" Allie asked as she shooed him away from the stove. "We're not sure. He went off somewhere with the bishop."

Saloma sat at the table and let out a small grunt, her way of needing attention. Reuben sat beside his mother, and Allie asked, "Tell us all about it. Were you able to get them to agree to stop the foreclosure?"

Reuben broke off a piece of cookie from the plate on the table. "We showed—" He stopped, hearing the crunch of gravel on the driveway outside. Moving to the window, he saw an old Jeep grind to a stop. "Who's that?" he muttered.

A tall, middle-aged, willowy brunette exited the car, slamming the door with an angry thud. Her long hair was pulled back in a tight ponytail, swinging violently as she marched toward the door.

"I'll go," Reuben said, popping the rest of the cookie in his mouth. He opened the door before the woman could knock, which put him face to face with the *Englisch* dressed woman.

"Hello, what can I do for you?" Reuben asked pleasantly enough.

The woman didn't seem to be in any mood for pleasantries. "I'm looking for Saloma Raber. Is this her place?"

"It is, but she's not well and is in no state for visitors."

The woman stood on her tippy toes and looked over his shoulder through the open door. "I don't care if she's up for visitors or not. I'm not leaving until I speak to her."

The woman made an unpleasant face at Reuben's response. "I think not. Like I said, she's not up for visitors. She's recovering from a stroke and doesn't need to be upset."

In a bold move, the woman pushed past him and into the kitchen, spewing her demands. "She'll be more than upset if you don't let me talk to her. I'm not putting up with her slandering threats a minute longer."

Reuben tried to grab her arm, but the woman twisted free, landing smack in front of Saloma. Instantly, in a protective manner, Allie moved to Saloma's side, resting her hand on Saloma's shoulder.

Pushing his way between them, Reuben barked, "I don't know what your story is, but you need to leave." Saloma reached over and tugged Reuben's shirt sleeve, nodding her approval for the woman to stay.

"What is this all about?" Allie snarled. "Who are you, and what business is so important that you're being rude?"

"Saloma and I were friends long ago," the woman hissed. "It's complicated."

"And that means what to her now?" Reuben inquired.

Allie piped in again, "Who are you?"

The woman took in a long-labored breath. "Janet McNeal...Mose Weaver's *schwester*."

Reuben looked toward his mother, and she gave him a faint, embittered nod when he asked if she knew her. "So again, what is this all about?" he asked.

There was a strange, unblinking look on Saloma's face. "*Mamm*, do you know what this is all about?" Reuben asked.

Janet looked at him quizzically. "Can't she talk?"

"*Nee*. She lost her voice to the stroke."

With a victorious laugh, Janet stated, "Well isn't that something? Here, I was worried for nothing. Can't do much damage if she can't even talk."

"What are you talking about? "Allie commanded.

"What do you think, Saloma? Should I share with your children what you've been up to? I assume this is Reuben's wife. The one you've tried so hard to ostracize at the cost of another child's family."

Allie turned toward her mother-in-law and watched as tears coursed down her cheeks. The look of brokenness touched a deep spot in Allie's heart, and she knelt. "*Mamm*, do you know what she's referring to?" Suddenly, *Gott* had given Allie what she'd been praying for. A tenderness and forgiving spirit toward her mother-in-law.

At that moment, it didn't matter. Standing to face Janet, Allie declared, "We have no desire to know what she may have done. My only concern is that you don't upset her any further."

"I'm not leaving until I set some things straight." Removing her outer jacket, Allie and Reuben gulped at the sight of her light jean jacket missing one of its brass buttons.

The side door swung open, and Mose hollered, "Janet, what are you doing here?"

Janet raised a brow. "What do you think I'm doing here? I'm saving your family a mess of embarrassment."

"I told you I would handle things." Mose groaned.

Daniel hobbled in the back door and moved to Saloma's side. "I'd say you have bigger things to concern yourself with."

"And what might that be?"

Daniel sat at the table and stretched out his leg, handing Reuben his crutches. "You can start by telling us why you were behind our barn."

"I...I don't know what you're talking about."

Mose moved in closer and pointed to where her jacket was missing a button. "I'd think twice about your answer, *schwester*."

Janet looked to where everyone was glaring. "So, I'm missing a button. What's that have to do with anything?"

"We found a button just like that in the mud alongside the rubble of the barn. No one around here wears buttons, and it looks like the one you're missing."

"So again," Daniel pressed, "why were you behind our barn, and was it you who started the fire?"

"No! I swear I had nothing to do with that. Yes, I was here the other night, but I had nothing to do with the fire. In fact, I ran back into the woods when I heard two men talking. It wasn't until the explosion threw me to the ground that I realized how close I'd come to dying in that fire."

Allie added, "We saw two men run from the barn that night. Did you get a good look at them?"

"No, it was too dark. I could only tell you they weren't Amish, and I think one of them drove a dark pickup truck. I saw it parked on the side of the road at the end of the lane when I left."

Daniel slapped his hand on the table. "Why should we believe you? You came here to cause trouble; how do we know you didn't start the fire before those two men arrived?"

Janet sank down into a chair. "I just wanted to scare Saloma into keeping her mouth closed. I was going to spray paint a message on the cider press. That's all, I promise."

Mose shook his head. "Janet, I wouldn't have permitted Saloma to carry out her threat. I would have done whatever it took to keep your secret, even if it meant revealing her plans to Reuben and Allie so they could stop her."

Hanging her head, Janet moaned. "I couldn't stand the thought of her revealing the truth. I didn't want your boy to think less of you because you kept my secret all these years."

She paused and looked at Daniel and Saloma. "I begged them not to tell him. I never wanted him to feel like he had a mother who didn't want him." Janet wiped her eyes with the back of her hand. "I was afraid every time I looked at him, I would see the face of the man who violated me." She sighed and continued. "As it is, every time I see a man with a scar on his face, I cringe."

The gut-wrenching intensity of the woman's voice left Allie reeling in compassion. "Did you go to the police? Did they catch him?"

She gasped. "Heavens no. I kept the whole incident to myself until I discovered I was with child. Only then did I confide in Catherine and Mose. I was a minor, and my parents would have had to be involved. Mose and I decided our parents weren't strong enough to withstand the shame of it all."

An alarming flash of anger fell on Mose's face, and he addressed Daniel and Reuben. "A dark truck, a scar? Could it be?"

Reuben quickly asked, "Janet, describe the man. What did he look like?"

She stuttered. "I don't remember much about him. I'm sure I blocked out most of it, but I'll always remember the scar that crawled down his chin onto his neck. It was red and ugly then, and I overheard him saying that he'd been in a fight in prison."

"So, you knew him?" Allie asked.

"I met him at a party that I shouldn't have been at," Janet confessed.

Mose bluntly added, "I believe justice is about to be served."

***

Reuben reached over and pulled Allie close after she turned the alarm off. "I don't want to get up. Can't we just lay here all morning?"

"That sounds nice, but your parents will want breakfast, and Almer will be pounding on the door any minute." She nestled her head on his shoulder and asked, "What's on your agenda today?"

"Lots," he sighed. "Clean up starts today. We must clear the cement pad to be ready when the community comes next week to build the cider barn. The lumber has already been ordered and should be delivered tomorrow." He kissed the top of her head. "And how about you?"

"Your mother was quite upset last night after Janet's visit. I wish the therapist was coming today. I need her to help me find a way for her to communicate with us. It's like she's in a box with no way out."

"I wouldn't change a thing about you, Mrs. Raber," Reuben said very quietly.

"Why?" she inquired.

"Look at how our life has played out in just a couple short months. Showing my mother grace through all this has made me love you even more. And all you've had to put up with from me. Plain and simple, you make me a better man."

"*Gott* desired me to go through your mother's disapproval to lean into Him more. Had I not endured that, I wouldn't have looked to him for strength."

Reuben couldn't help but hug her tenderly. He felt he was the luckiest man alive to find a woman who would sacrifice her own wishes and desires to care for his...at times...difficult family. Only one thing was missing, and he knew it was time to approach the conversation.

Resting his hand against their growing child, he asked, "Allie, we must discuss church. I've made a few decisions, and I hope you'll agree with my attentions."

"*Jah?*"

"I've spoken to Bishop Weaver and Bishop Schrock from the New Order Fellowship. I've also sought council with some of my *bruders*."

There was a calming assurance in Allie's tone. "And what did you decide?"

"It's not what I've decided; it's what we need to decide together. But I hope you'll agree to join the New Order Fellowship."

"Reuben, on this subject, I will follow your direction and do whatever you feel is best for our family."

"I think the Old Order is too strict and will be too much of a change for you."

"But it's your heritage. How can I ask you to walk away from that?"

"You're not asking me to walk away from anything, and trust me, I've prayed a lot about this. I think a more liberal church where we're encouraged to step out in faith is where *Gott* is leading us."

"But your parents and most *bruders* are still part of the Old Order. Won't that cause issues between us?"

Reuben sat up, swung his feet over the edge of the bed, and pondered her question. It wasn't until Allie snuggled up behind him and wrapped her arms around his neck that he got his answer. "It's not that we won't still value the things that are important to my Amish upbringing; it's just that the New Order will allow us to develop a personal relationship with Jesus in a much more open manner."

Allie hugged him tighter. "My mother told me once that what you are devoted to will end up shaping you." She leaned in closer and whispered in his ear, "What more could a woman want than to have her husband chase after the Lord?"

He grabbed her hands and pulled her around to his lap. "Bishop Schrock told me that growth requires sacrifice and adjustments. That statement has stayed with me for days. Allie, I want this for us and our family."

"Then that's what I want too."

Allie nodded toward the dress and *kap*p hanging on the peg by the door. "Does that mean I don't have to wear those?"

"Not unless you want to," he said with a twinkling eye.

"I'd much prefer not to, then."

"Bishop Schrock mentioned that a new couple moved into the district and started to attend the church. He's hoping we can reach out to them and make them feel welcome. He feels you will be perfect for her since she is new to the Amish community as well."

"Really? How wonderful. Do you know their names?"

"Not sure, but they moved here from Charleston, South Carolina. He said they have family in the area, and he comes from an Amish background. Sounds like we have a good bit in common with them."

"Oh, Reuben, that tickles me. I can't wait to meet them."

"Then it's settled. I'll let Bishop Schrock know we'll be attending on Sunday, and I'll have a talk with my parents so there are no expectations otherwise."

***

Daniel and Saloma were already in the kitchen when Allie made it downstairs. Daniel had all their papers strewed out across the table, and Saloma was attempting to make coffee with one hand. A quick surge of disappointment surfaced when Allie saw him studying the new proposals for the event barn. It had been weeks since they spoke of her ideas, and she tried to push away her distress.

He waved her over. "I have some questions about the new kitchen and store layout. I'm considering connecting the event barn with the cider mill area and separating it with glass so our visitors can watch the cider being made. What do you think?"

Confused by his sudden open interest, she was shocked when she got a confirming nod from Saloma. Moved by their acceptance, it touched something inside of her that she attributed to another answered prayer.

"I think that's a perfect idea," was all she could get out before a blinding wish to cry brought on unashamed tears.

Saloma scuffled to her side using her cane, then, lowering herself to a chair at the table. Daniel handed Allie a box of tissues as Reuben walked into the kitchen.

"*Mamm,* what did you do now?" Reuben asked, with some exasperation.

"Allie, why are you crying?"

"Sit down, son; there are a few things your mother and I want to talk to you both about."

"That's good because Allie and I also have a few things."

Daniel cleared his throat. "If you don't mind, I'd like to start." It took a few minutes for him to gather his thoughts before he began. "Something happens to a man when he has to give up control of everything and rely on his children for the most menial chores."

"*Datt,* that's what family is for."

"Let me finish." Daniel sipped his coffee and continued. "We haven't been able to do much but sit in our chairs and watch, listen, and surrender. We observed you both coming to our rescue without hesitation. I've listened to Allie share her ideas on saving Raber Farms, and we've had to surrender everything to *Gott's* will."

A silence filled the room as they waited for Daniel to steady his voice. "During that time, *Gott* worked on our hearts and brought a few things to light. One is that a broken relationship cannot be reunited until the offender asks for forgiveness. And this needs to be a two-way street, as we all have said and done things to harm one another."

Allie sucked in a breath, and a sob released, forcing Reuben to squeeze her hand. Even Saloma seemed genuinely moved as what Allie thought may be tears of remorse filled her eyes.

"Your mother and I want to ask for your forgiveness. We seek peace."

Saloma began to whimper softly and, in a throaty voice, whispered, "I'm so...sorry."

"*Mamm*, your voice!" Allie exclaimed.

Daniel reached over, laid his hand over Saloma's, and declared, "Just another miracle among many."

"Among many?" Reuben asked.

"*Jah*. Allie is the miracle your mother has prayed for."

Allie turned toward Saloma. "Me?"

Daniel nodded. "All she's ever wanted was a daughter to share life with. When all the other girls rejected her after she pushed too hard to be in control, it took her losing her voice and relying on you for everything to realize *Gott* had answered her prayer."

No longer capable of feeling anything but compassion and no words to describe her thankfulness, Allie stood and wrapped her arms around both their shoulders, pulling them both in close. Their stiffness melted at her open show of emotion the longer she held them, and Saloma muttered, "Thank you."

After they all settled back in their chairs and Allie started to fix breakfast, Daniel added, "There is one more thing we'd like to talk about."

"What's that?" Reuben asked as he stirred cream and sugar in his coffee.

"It's time for us to leave this farmhouse and hand it over to you and Allie. We will move into the *doddi haus* as soon as Saloma feels up to it."

Reuben drew in a worried sigh. "So soon? You're still so young."

"If I've learned nothing else through the last few months, it's to trust in the Lord's plan and timetable. He forced us to slow down and rely on Him. And during that time, the Lord has impressed on me it's time."

"But what if I decide to go back into furniture making? I may not want to continue here."

"Reuben, whatever you decide is fine with us." Daniel grinned and looked over at Allie. "You, on the other hand, don't have a choice. Without you and your ideas, I can't move forward with these designs."

Allie felt a sudden rousing of kinship and answered, "I'm not going anywhere. I have a notebook full of ideas dying to be released."

Daniel snorted a belly laugh. "Then I guess we'd better get started."

EPILOGUE

Five months later

A swarm of honeybees clung to a low-hanging branch of the tree outside the kitchen window. On a gentle breeze, the sweet smell of apple blossoms blew through the open screen door, and Allie rubbed her swollen belly as she watched the fury of activity.

Reuben approached behind her and wrapped his arms around her middle, letting his big hand rest across her stomach. "Not much longer, *jah*?"

"Not soon enough for me," she moaned. Labor was slow and agonizing; it was all she could do to move, let alone walk around as her midwife suggested. When the pain doubled her over, she let Reuben support her weight as she breathed through the spasm. Regaining her posture, she cried, "I know I said I wanted to do this alone, but I need your *mamm*. Will you go get her?"

After helping her to a chair, he quickly added, "*Mamm* didn't want to be too far away, so she's in the store pricing inventory."

Picking up one of the newly designed Raber Farm brochures from the table, she smiled at how her in-laws let her hire her new friend, Savannah, to help with marketing. Because of that, they were able to open Raber's Amish Farm Store four months earlier than planned.

With Daniel's plan of selling shares of the farm, all their Amish neighbors helped in a big way. The store and event facility were the first to be completed, and they already had weddings and events booked way into next year. A few families even took it upon themselves to offer Amish Farm Dinners, allowing groups to take advantage of homecooked Amish meals.

After all they had gone through the previous year, it seemed *Gott* was blessing everything they touched, especially since they weren't shy about giving *Gott* all the glory.

Allie's idea to make Raber Farms a destination venue revitalized the community and breathed new life into the dying farming industry. More and more cottage businesses were popping up as Amish tourism rose. Those Amish families with products to sell took advantage of the store to sell their wares.

As another wave of contractions took over, Allie looked out over the beehive and tried calming her breathing by concentrating on the humming. She couldn't help but think about all the changes that had taken place in the Raber household since she came along. Like the queen bee, Saloma had complete control of her hive and kept it busy doing her bidding, regardless of the cost.

They would not have found a renewed relationship with the Lord, family, and their community without their traumatic year. It took life's challenges to remind them what was important to a family.

As the tightening eased, she walked to the window and watched Saloma walk with Reuben across the yard. She was never one to believe in miracles, but a complete transformation took place in her mother-in-law that could only come from the Lord.

Lifting up a prayer of thanksgiving, she was now less concerned about what it took to please people than what it took to please *Gott*. But mostly, she learned that family peace was the direct result of family struggles, and she'd be forever grateful for that.

Savannah's

Amish Ties That Bind

THE AMISH WOMEN OF
LAWRENCE COUNTY SERIES - BOOK 6

Tracy Fredrychowski

Tracy Fredrychowski

PROLOGUE
Charleston, South Carolina

I remember the day I first laid eyes on Neal Carmichael. I'd been trying to maneuver a large box up three flights of stairs when he took it from my hands and delivered it to the third-floor apartment, taking the steps two at a time.

Over the next few weeks, I watched him from my upstairs window like clockwork. Twice a day, he would carry his bike outside and disappear into Charleston, South Carolina's busy cobblestone streets. I never knew where he went but found myself holding my breath until he returned.

There was something different about him—something about the way he carried himself suggested there was more to him than what met the eye. And what met the eye was quite appealing. Aside from his sandy blonde hair, which he kept perfectly shaped, and his wide-set eyes that looked like a clear summer day, I only knew he lived on the first floor and rode his bike everywhere he went.

He had the sweetest accent on the rare occasion he spoke or at least acknowledged my existence. His tone carried a gentle lilt, each syllable pronounced with care, as if dictating English wasn't his first language. When I questioned his nationality, his brilliant blue eyes expressed aloofness as he replied, "American."

Confused and lost in the melodic cadence of his words, I tucked his response away and inquired about the weather instead.

"Is it always this hot in April?"

He swung a long leg over his tapered bicycle and waved as he took off down the street, replying to my question. "Wouldn't know. Only been here a few months."

With temperatures already hovering near eighty degrees, I watched him become a fading figure in the Charleston landscape. I still felt the breeze that carried the perfume from the Carolina Jessamine outside our apartment building that morning. Had I known the pain I would have endured by pursuing him, I would have walked away that balmy spring morning, never to look back.

And I, Savannah Carmichael, now unemployed marketing executive, was packing boxes in my posh Ashley River condo without knowing where my husband was or if he was ever coming home. I had no choice but to return to my grandmother's Willow Springs, Pennsylvania home. The home—and I use the word loosely—had been left to her by my mother, and its upkeep had been mainly ignored.

I often spoke to my grandmother on the phone but ignored her invitations to visit on more than one occasion. Her eccentric manner and simple living tendencies went against my stylish, high-living expectations for my life.

I had only visited my Gigi, as she liked to be called, on a few occasions. Even though my parents lived on the shores of Lake Erie, less than an hour away, we rarely visited.

While I knew she loved me, and I could always count on her to give me sound advice, especially after my parents died, there was something mysterious about her. Something I could never quite place. She enjoyed life like no one I'd ever known. Even after Poppy passed, she found joy in the simplest things. Mom said it was because she spent too much time with her Amish neighbors. But Dad said she kept her nose buried in the bible so much she lost all sense of reality.

Regardless, all I have to look forward to now is a run-down house on the edge of town with a peculiar grandmother with whom I don't have anything in common. And now, after the disturbing realization that my husband of three years has come up missing with no traceable explanation, along with my dream job being eliminated, I'm forced to leave this beautiful city behind. It wasn't how I had planned to spend my morning, let alone my life.

Read more about Savannah in the sixth book of
The Amish Women of Lawrence County Series.
Savannah's Amish Ties That Bind

WHAT DID YOU THINK?

First of all, thank you for purchasing *The Amish Women of Lawrence County – Allie's Amish Family Miracle*. I hope you will enjoy all the books in this series.

You could have picked any number of books to read, but you chose this book, and for that, I am incredibly grateful. I hope it added value and quality to your everyday life. If so, it would be nice to share this book with your friends and family on social media.

If you enjoyed this book and found some benefit in reading it, I'd like to hear from you and hope that you could take some time to post a review on Amazon. Your feedback and support will help me improve my writing craft for future projects.

If you loved visiting Willow Springs, I invite you to sign up for my private email list, where you'll get to explore more of the characters of this Amish Community.

Sign up at https://dl.bookfunnel.com/v9wmnj7kve and download the novella that starts this series, *The Amish Women of Lawrence County*.

GLOSSARY

Pennsylvania Dutch "Deutsch" Words

Ausbund. Amish songbook.

bruder. Brother

datt. Father or dad.

denki. Thank You.

doddi. Grandfather.

doddi haus. A small house next to the main house.

g'may. Community

goot meiya. Good morning.

jah. Yes.

kapp. Covering or prayer cap.

kinner. Children.

mamm. Mother or mom.

grossmommi. Grandmother.

nee. No.

Ordnung. Order or set of rules the Amish follow.

schwester. Sister.

singeon. Singing/youth gathering.

The Amish are a religious group typically referred to as Pennsylvania Dutch, Pennsylvania Germans, or Pennsylvania Deutsch. They are descents of early German immigrants to Pennsylvania, and their beliefs center around living a conservative lifestyle. They arrived between the late 1600s and the early 1800s to escape religious persecutions in Europe. They first settled in Pennsylvania with the promise of religious freedom by William Penn. Most Pennsylvania Dutch still speak a variation of their original German language as well as English.

ABOUT THE AUTHOR

Tracy Fredrychowski lives a life similar to the stories she writes. Striving to simplify her life, she often shares her simple living tips and ideas on her website and blog at https://tracyfredrychowski.com.

Growing up in rural northwestern Pennsylvania, country living was instilled in her from an early age. As a young woman, she was traumatized by the murder of a young Amish woman in her rural Pennsylvania community. She became dedicated to sharing stories of their simple existence. She inspires her readers to live Gott-centered lives through faith, family, and community. If you want to enjoy more of the Amish of Lawrence County, she invites you to join her on Facebook. There she shares her friend Jim Fisher's Amish photography, recipes, short stories, and an inside look at her favorite Amish community nestled in northwestern Pennsylvania, deep in Amish Country.

Facebook.com/tracyfredrychowskiauthor/

Facebook.com/groups/tracyfredrychowski/